D0904382

MAKE THAT SCENE

Books by William Noble

"Shut Up!" He Explained, Middlebury, Vermont, 1987
Steal This Plot (with June Noble), Middlebury, Vermont, 1985
The Psychiatric Fix (with June Noble), New York, 1981
The Private Me (with June Noble), New York, 1980
How to Live With Other People's Children (with June Noble), New York, 1978
The Custody Trap (with June Noble), New York, 1975

MAKE THAT SCENE

A Writer's Guide to
Setting, Mood and Atmosphere

by
William Noble

Paul S. Eriksson
PUBLISHER
MIDDLEBURY, VT 05753

FIRST TRADE PAPERBACK EDITION

Manufactured in the United States of America

10 9 8 7 6 5 4 3 2 1

Library of Congress Cataloging-in-Publication Data

Noble, William.
   Make that scene: a writer's guide to setting, mood, and atmosphere/by William Noble.
p.   cm.

   Bibliography: p.
   Includes index
   ISBN 0-8397-5708-5: $17.95 (Cloth)
   1. Authorship. 2. Setting (Literature) I. Title.
PN218.N628 1988
808' .02-dc 19

                                              88-19198
                                              CIP

ISBN 0-8397-5709-3 (Paperback)

For My Patti

Contents

MAKE THAT SCENE

Preface

Where Am I?

It is three weeks into the term and my writing students are handing in their first piece of assigned fiction. For some it represents an arduous effort brimming with uncertainty and unexpected reactions—I never thought I'd write about *that*... this is fun!...God, I've led a dull life!... I'm confused...

Their faces mirror their sentiments, and as I collect the stories, I say, "Relax, I don't expect publishable material at this stage."

"Mine isn't even readable!" comes an unhappy voice.

There's a ripple of nervous laughter. "How many wrote about something familiar?

"Something we know, you mean?"

I nod.

"From experience?"

I nod again.

3

"Books?"

"Stories from my grandmother?" (laughter)

"TV...?"

"Personal experience is best."

"Is there an alternative?" I ask.

"How about making it all up?"

I've been through this with other classes. There is nothing inherently wrong about writing fiction when it's totally the figment of our imaginations, but sometimes it makes the writing task much more difficult. Everything must be invented, and our level of familiarity—without a good deal of research—is likely limited to clichés and overworked situations.

The initial step in understanding why we should fall back on something familiar is to look at the locale of our story— the picture frame within which we weave the action. It had better be a picture frame we know well.

"Where do you set your story?" I ask a student.

"In a police precinct house."

A mystery story, then?"

"Suspense and murder, drugs and bad guys." A couple of low whistles from other students.

"You ever been in a police precinct house?" I ask.

A slow shake of the head. "I read a lot."

"You ever held a kilo of cocaine?"

"No."

"You ever seen a dead body?"

"No."

"You know what records the police have to keep on confiscated drugs?"

"I can guess."

"Sometimes guessing makes it seem unreal, unauthentic."

I smile at the student. "I'm making a point, I think."

"Any chance I could get my story back before you read it?" He's gotten my point.

I speak to the entire class. "My point is...?"

A soft response from the front row. "Knowing your setting?" I nod, encouraging more... "Think of capital letters, underlines, exclamation points..."

"KNOW YOUR SETTING!"

"You've got it," I say.

The cardinal principle when we set a story is to be familiar —most familiar—with the locale of what we're writing about. My student had had little contact with the setting of the story and so the clichés, the overworked situations flood the mind and ultimately the storyline. What we know is sometimes *not* what we are familiar with; an effective scene can best result when what we know and are familiar with become the same thing.

Take my student. Unfamiliarity with the scene might cause the desk sergeant at the precinct house to be described:

...beefy, heavy jowled, slumping behind the thick wooden desk, intent on the sports section of the morning paper...

A portrait of disinterest which tells us the setting will be unappealing. To any reader of police procedurals, this is an overworked description, a cliché-laden scene.

The real situation in the real precinct house is much different. The desk sergeant (who most likely will be behind a glass partition now) must be alert, a commanding figure, because this is often the first exposure to police authority the public has, and it had better set an effective tone. The desk sergeant (or in many cases an assigned patrolman or patrolwoman) is the most visible member of the precinct-house police. Other police officials walk by constantly, the phones are ringing, there is a steady babble. The desk person had better be someone who is both alert *and* talented enough to handle a myriad of problems, expected and unexpected.

Wouldn't this read better?

...dark-eyed, quiet spoken, a sheaf of reports in her hand, she leaned over the computer terminal and waited for a response to her question...

Knowing our setting means understanding it as well as describing it, and understanding only comes with familiarity. To some writers this means tasting it, smelling it, involving oneself to the point where the setting of a story is as intimate to creator and reader as the birthmark on the buttocks of a character.

Familiarity, deep familiarity.

Here are Robie Macauley and George Lanning, a generation ago, discussing setting as a fiction technique. Things haven't changed:

Writers who stick to familiar ground are less prone to irrelevant detail than those who go afield. When dealing with the unfamiliar, writers respond too often as any tourist does. They carry away masses of what might be called public information—the picture-postcard things that everyone sees...

There was an editor who set a simple standard for good fiction. He believed that four questions had to be answered in the first few pages of a novel, and if they weren't answered, he read no further:

—what happened?
—to whom did it happen?
—when did it happen? (the time boundary)
—where did it happen? (the place boundary)

Each of these bears on the setting of a story, though the latter two have a greater impact. The important thing, however, is to realize that each of these questions must be answered *early* in the story, in the first few pages, and that the questions all reflect:

Where am I?

See how Booth Tarkington in *The Magnificent Ambersons* answers this question on the first page of the novel:

In that town, in those days, all the women who wore silk or velvet knew all the other women who wore silk or velvet, and when there was a new purchase of sealskin, sick people were taken to windows to see it go by. Trotters were out, in the winter afternoons, racing light sleighs on National Avenue and Tennessee Street; everybody recognized both the trotters and the drivers; and again knew them as well on summer evenings when slim buggies whizzed by in renewals of the snow-time rivalry...

A town small enough so that people with the same tastes and characteristics couldn't hide from one another, a town large enough so there was vivid class-consciousness. From these few lines a reader could gather the atmosphere of the town, as well as its general locale. The reader knows exactly where he/she is.

Details become important because they give the reader a peg to identify with, to fasten on to the action. The setting comes alive when the details evoke a reaction such as "... of course! That's the way it should look or smell or sound..." The reader is a participant, not just an observer. But the use of detail must be carefully apportioned; it cannot overwhelm the other aspects of the story. For example, a room could be described:

... high ceilinged, with rococo molding a foot from the top of the wall, stretching in an unbroken line round the four walls, overseeing seven chairs and one couch spread in a loose square, end tables positioned exactly, the wood highly polished, ashtrays centered on each table, decanters within easy reach, tapestries of rich reds, greens and browns hanging decorously from the thick stone walls...

Or the room could be described:

largish and light-filled, faintly smelling of pipe smoke, thick, country-home chairs and couch well polished, the coldness from the stone walls subdued by rich tapestries...

One half the space to say the same thing, and the reader isn't forced to wade through a bog of detail. The art of scene setting comes not from detail dropping itself but from judicious dropping of *certain* details—those that can portray the scene in the most vivid terms. Here's novelist Mary Stewart on the subject:

A physical setting should never be built up too elaborately... For example, nothing is worse than reading a detailed description of a room. Something of the size and style and color and perhaps three telling details are all that is necessary...

Note the above example. Size, style and color (largish, country-home, light-filled), three telling details... smelling of pipe smoke, polished furniture, tapestries on the cold walls.

Do we need much more? Can the action now proceed?

Setting serves a variety of purposes, and the accomplished writer uses and reuses them in order to establish authenticity and a sense of drama in the story. Setting is not a static device that can be fastened on a scene without a close awareness of what its consequences will be. At the same time, though, setting must be utilized thoroughly enough so that a proper sense of *where am I?* can affect the reader. In general, setting should be considered for use in the following ways:

   —to add vividness to the story; an unforgettable background will make the characters stand out and be memorable. The sea stories of Joseph Conrad are one example of this, the struggles of poor-white existence in William Faulkner's works are another.

   —to influence character; where a person lives, grows up or has telling experiences will often determine the way he/she thinks or acts. F. Scott Fitzgerald's Gatsby is an example of this, as are the urban - oriented novels of Phillip Roth.

   —to play a role in the story; where the setting is so powerful it can become an actual character in the story, it can even dominate the characters. Some of Edgar Alan Poe's work—especially *The Fall of the House of Usher*—would come in here, as would William Golding's *Lord of the Flies*.

These uses for setting can be woven and interwoven so that matters never remain stationary. For example, we set a story so the action is played against a harsh environment, man against nature... then, suddenly, the teamwork of the characters dissolves, and one character (or more) becomes a menace to the others because he or she believes the harsh environment will swallow them all:

He watched them through the night, convinced now they would dump him over the side as soon as he sank into an exhausted sleep. Twenty-six feet of floating survival, eight mouths to feed, thousands of ocean

9

> miles, empty, unforgiving... he hated them all, uneducated, conniving, cruel, they'd never be rescued...

Setting, then, is the result of the writer's using his or her experience and knowledge to create a locale for the story, and the technique for developing this is through the use of descriptive phrases and details which provide a picture to the reader.

But then there's atmosphere.

Atmosphere goes hand in glove with setting. One without the other is like a painting without a frame or a frame without a painting. Atmosphere (or mood) is what the reader feels as the effect of the setting settles. It is the writer's way of injecting life into the stiff details of the locale. "Atmosphere," according to Peggy Simson Curry, "is the result of presenting the physical details in such a way as to create emotional reaction."

Emotional reaction in the story. Important goal, and the reason is obvious. Emotional reaction is what allows the reader to identify and empathize.

See how Walter Van Tilburg Clark in *The Wind and the Snow of Winter* develops his story atmosphere from a judicious use of setting details. Note, too, how the mood of Mike, an old gold miner heading into town as winter comes, contrasts with the setting itself:

> It was getting darker rapidly in the pass. When a gust of wind brought the snow against Mike's face so hard that he noticed the flakes felt larger, he looked up. The light was still there, although the fire was dying out of it, and the snow swarmed across it more thickly. Mike remembered God. He did not think anything exact. He did not think about his own relationship to

God. He merely felt the idea as a comforting presence. He'd always had a feeling about God whenever he looked at a sunset, especially a sunset which came through a stormy sky...

In spite of the raging weather and the nearness of winter, Mike feels and projects comfort, as if he is above the tempest. The atmosphere and the mood of the story are generated by Mike's thoughts, and as we see, he is at peace with the elements even though they storm about him. In Peggy Simson Curry's words, the atmosphere of contentment is the result of his slogging through the snow and wind. The rough weather merely affords him a chance to seek calmness—it "creates" the emotional reaction.

We can apply this type of cause and effect in other circumstances: a crowded, bustling street creates torment, perhaps even terror... a moonlit night in balmy weather creates a love-filled heart... a tawdry, run down rooming house creates suspicion, even paranoia...

The point is the physical setting becomes the picture frame within which the emotional reaction blooms.

Mood and atmosphere (the terms are really interchangeable, except to a purist, and for our purposes purists are mostly confined behind the walls of academia) are integral to all the parts of a story; they depend on plot, on the characters, on the style the writer uses. Each aspect of the story will influence the mood and atmosphere, each will provide some basis for an emotional reaction. A story set, for example, on a luxury cruise ship could have a plot steeped in mystery and death; the emotional reactions would certainly include fear and terror even in the midst of glorious wealth. The plot itself influences the emotions of the characters, and the plot, in turn, is a creature of the setting—the cruise ship.

It works this way with characterization, too. See how Virginia Woolf, in *Mrs. Dalloway,* portrays segments of the British class system and in doing it also develops a definite story mood:

> The crush was terrific for the time of day. Lords, Ascot, Hurlingham, what was it? she wondered, for the street was blocked. The British middle classes sitting sideways on the tops of omnibuses with parcels and umbrellas, yes, even furs on a day like this, were, she thought, more ridiculous, more unlike anything there has ever been than one could conceive; and the Queen herself held up; the Queen herself unable to pass. Clarissa was suspended on one side of Brook Street; Sir John Buckhurst, the old Judge, on the other, with the car between them (Sir John had laid down the law for years and liked a well-dressed woman) when the chauffeur, leaning ever so slightly, said or showed something to the policeman, who saluted and raised his arm and jerked his head and moved the omnibus to the side and the car passed through...

The hauteur of the judge, the silliness of the British middle classes are all part of the setting here, and the fact that the Queen is caught in the traffic jam only lends another dimension to the scene. In fact who would think a Queen could be bottled up in something so ordinary as a traffic jam? The Queen is as mortal as the citizens sitting on top of the omnibus in furs and with their parcels. In this short passage we have a strong portrait of British society painted against the framework of a simple street scene. By setting forth the scene Virginia Woolf portrays a mood of class consciousness and its sillier aspects.

Character build-up can equal mood creation. Try it...

—An imperious financier addresses the board of directors of a company he wishes to take over the mood is conflict and fury.

—An inept waiter attempts to serve a demanding table. The more he tries, the more disaster looms—the mood is frenzied laughter.

Simple, really.

Suppose we come face to face with nonfiction? Does it affect how we use setting, mood and atmosphere? The clear answer is no... fact or fiction make little difference. The picture frame and the emotional reaction it creates adhere to the same rules. See how Theodore Plievier in his book *Stalingrad,* a recreation of the famous battle, describes what a German lieutenant, Lawkow, sees as he retreats across a plain of darkened snow:

> On the following day the peaceful skiing terrain had become a very unpleasant deployment area for Russian tanks; firing blazed on the heights and in the little grove of trees and Lawkow realized again that he was nothing but a grain of dust. But luck was with this grain of dust; he had crossed the Tartar Wall a second time and come again into the familiar chaos—guns, hordes of limping men, and more Russian heavy tanks rolling over trucks and suitcases, over a group of screaming men, cutting off another group. There were five, six tanks on the broad expanse of snow. The hatches flew open and on tanks one, two and three a Russian officer popped up, a submachine gun in his hand...

The setting is a battlefield, the mood and atmosphere death and destruction, all as recorded by the eye of Lieutenant

Lawkow. This book is clearly nonfiction (though written in novelistic form), but note the dramatic effect the setting creates. There is tension, drama, ultimate conflict—the same requisites that a good fiction scene demands. The author, himself, provides us with a glimpse of how he went about writing it all, and in so doing shows that good scene-setting can be equally at home in nonfiction or fiction:

> I saw the battlefields myself; in my own hands I held those wretched records taken from the dead bodies on the battlefields—the letters and diaries; and I spoke myself with the war prisoners, officers and men; and I undertook to describe what happened on the Volga...

The important thing to note is this: setting, mood and atmosphere arise out of the details in the scene, *not* out of whether those details are representations of fact or fiction. Good writing can create a word-picture for the reader, and that, after all, is what making a scene is all about.

Where am I?

Sometimes the answer rests not with inanimate objects or with landscape or with character development. Sometimes the answer is in the portrayal of action...what's happening tells us where we are. It's the ultimate melding of plot with setting, mood and atmosphere. And it's a good technique. See how Joyce Carol Oates does it with her novel *You Must Remember This,* the story of a former prize fighter, Felix Stevick, now managing a younger man, Jo-Jo Pearl. Here's Jo-Jo's big fight against a former champion, and Felix is there:

> He hadn't seen Jo-Jo fight for nearly two months so it was a relief to note that the boy was at the top of his form; less brash than Felix remembered but still belligerent, pushy, circling his opponent and rushing

him with brief volleys that seemed spurred in part by the audience's impatience. In the stark bright overhead lights Jo-Jo's handsome face was carefully without expression, his body quick, urgent, lithe. He was taller than McCord by perhaps two inches and lighter by six pounds though his torso was now well developed with muscle, his neck somewhat thick. By contrast McCord looked paunchy and uncoordinated, swinging crudely, not minding that he missed his target, standing flat-footed and swinging again, head ducked down, knees bent, showing Jo-Jo a dull dogged beady-eyed look of malice...

This is part of a five-page scene, and it is almost devoid of description about the arena, the ring, the spectators—the usual details that spice up a fight scene. But Oates limits herself to the fighters themselves, describing them and the action, including the physical damage each sustains as the fight progresses. In this she is using the action as the setting, allowing us to understand that what is happening really tells us where we are.

The fighters fight, they move and circle and hit and cover up...

Do we need to know the spectators are screaming or the arena is smoke-filled or the beer vendors are doing big business? Do we need to know that a small pocket of gamblers offers ever-changing odds as the fight progresses, or that a big-busted blonde is on her knees searching for a dropped earring as the action in the ring goes on?

Details, details. The fighters are the setting, they are the framework of the scene. Anything else would add little.

Where am I?

Fighting in the center of the ring.

Part A

Setting

Prelude

The beginning of any story is both the easiest and the most difficult place to be—easiest because we are not bound to any pre-created notions or circumstances, difficult because we must now unravel the entire tale without the support of an already established story line. Every story moves in the direction the beginning dictates: "it was..."" means something has happened in the past that will now be translated into present or future activity, "it is..." means that what has been going on is still going on, and the story picks up the activity, "it will be..." means future events will influence or control what is or has been going on.

In short, the start of a story sculpts the mold in which the work of art will take form and substance.

So it is with setting. We alluded to the idea of a picture frame as the creative boundary for where and how we set a story, and this is most appropriate. Imagine a tale set on an island, dark doings taking place, no relief from the mainland. The island, of course, is the setting, and the action, the character development, the story resolution flow from the setting. It is where things begin, it is what influences characters to act in certain ways, it is why the story exists in the first place. Without the island there would be no story, at least not a story like this!

Setting is best understood as an objective tool (in contrast to mood and atmosphere which are considered subjective tools—but more about these later). It is objective in that we experience its effect as spectators, not as participants. It is a look-see at surroundings from a neutral, disinterested point of view, not an attempt to envelope us in the feelings of the individual characters.

That doesn't mean effective portrayal of setting can't move us or bring us an appreciation of good writing technique. Look no further than Joseph Conrad's sea stories to see that even as Conrad describes a sea scene, we admire his descriptions, not only for their authenticity, but for the drama they invoke. The writing is "external" in the sense that the views of the sea can belong to the author and not to any particular character.

Setting *is* description. That doesn't mean it must be narrative, but it must create a scene. Dialogue, for example, is a perfectly appropriate tool for scene-setting:

"Five minutes into this publisher's party, and I'm bored."

"If it was your book you wouldn't be bored."

"If it was *my* book, we'd have the party at Twenty-One instead of this Soho loft."...

We know the party's in a less-than-exquisite part of town,

we know one of the characters is less than thrilled to be there, and we know these people are in the writing business. The scene is set in just three dialogue passages, description has been interwoven, and we know where we are.

Never forget that setting is a writer's *tool,* it is a technique for establishing something definite in the reader's mind. If he or she is confused about where we are, the story itself will trail off into nothingness. If we don't use setting to some purpose (such as plot development, characterization or conflict resolution), it will act as a weight-filled blob on the action. Setting must *do* something for the storyline... it must move it in some way.

For example, if we describe a street scene in a rundown section of a town, and then have all the action take place somewhere else, the setting has no influence on the action. It amounts to a snapshot without purpose. Now if we have the action take place in a boarded-up house on this street or in a sewer underneath this street, we don't have to allude to the street scene itself to understand why there are no amenities available. The setting explains it.

The key to setting lies in knowing how much to portray, how much to leave out. In the nineteenth century the French novelist, Honoré de Balzac, could take three or four pages to describe one room, but today we'd lose our readers if we attempted it. By the nature of things in our modern world, we expect quicker, more capsulated experiences, and when it comes to describing a single room, we'll take a few lines, perhaps even a few words only... thank you very much!

The point is this: we can get the flavor of the setting from a light touch of description, we don't need to pour it out (think of a béarnaise sauce... too much tarragon and the entire flavor is overpowered). Setting comes from the creation of an honest word-picture, one that provides us a framework much more than a monolithic platform. We need to know *something* of where our story springs from, but we don't need to know everything!

In the same way, we have to be careful with what we find out about the setting we use. Too much information is as harmful as too little information—both can tip the scene off balance. Knowing our setting is crucial, of course, but there's an art to transforming a jumble of facts into something meaningful. We need to learn when it's important to highlight facts we know, when it's important to trust to an unfailing imagination. A setting which combines both is a setting which will launch a string of bravos!

In the chapters to follow we'll see how scene-setting moves through the various phases I've described, from using details to developing a plot line or a characterization. It provides the grounding that every story needs and from which every story proceeds.

Setting is description; it must do something.

Just watch.

1

Creating a "Sense of Place"

The earliest memory I have is sitting atop a huge dark horse on a cold sunny day somewhere in a city. Years later, my parents show me a photo, tinged with brownish age.

"That's you," my mother says. "In Central Park."

Bare branches and indistinct buildings fill the background. I'm round faced and grinning, swathed in heavy clothes. A sober-faced policeman stands alongside, holding me upright with one hand. The horse stares balefully at the camera, his reins in the policeman's other hand.

"You weren't quite two, then," my mother says. "We moved from the city not long after."

My beginning years as a New Yorker, the earliest memories of what I was and what I became... perhaps. Am I the product of my birth and earliest memories? Is this where I find the grounding to produce what I produce today?

Does my "sense of place" shoot back to the years about which I remember almost nothing?

The answer, I think, has to be yes. We can't escape where we are born, nor where we grow up, any more than we can escape the fact we have blue eyes or large hands. These things influence what we do and how we do it. A New Yorker I am (though I hardly remember the two years we lived there), and somehow I judge other cities, other populations by what I have come to learn about New York. The weakness of my conscious memory has little to do with my sense of my own beginning, and in this I have created my own foundation. It has become the setting for the rest of my life to play out.

This doesn't mean, of course, that I can't settle comfortably in another town or city or dwell in another type of life; what it does mean is that wherever I go and whatever I do, I will take the baggage of my earliest New York impressions with me... streets and odors and crowds and colors and speech... and somehow they will find their way to influence what I write.

It is my sense of place, my setting.

Every writer has it, and every writer should recognize that the earliest experiences and memories play a part in what is written and how it is written. "The place of one's birth," according to J. Markus, "becomes as inevitable a fact of one's destiny as one's parents, one's genes."

As a New Yorker I would have difficulty writing about early years on a farm... but I have little trouble placing myself in the middle of the city and describing a crowded street scene or a rollicking ride on a smelly, screeching subway train.

My sense of place is natural, it's comfortable for me.

And that's the point. Writers develop their sense of place, and they recognize its influence when they create a piece of work. For example:

—Would Philip Roth's novels be so acutely urban if he hadn't been born in Newark, New Jersey?

—Would Nadine Gordimer's work be so poignantly anti-Apartheid if she hadn't been born in South Africa?

For all of us a sense of place is crucial because by developing it, we come to understand what we know best and what it will take for our characters and storyline to stand out.

What then does it take to make up a "sense of place"? Robie Macauley and George Lanning put it this way: "... it is the mountains or hills or plains, the houses people live in, the streets of a town or city, the quality of local life."

True enough, and we can see it in this excerpt from Sherwood Anderson's *Winesburg Ohio,* written many years ago. The book is a compilation of stories about the make-believe town, each one dealing with a different character and different events, though there are a couple of common threads running throughout. Note the sense of place Anderson evokes here as he opens a chapter in the middle of the book:

Snow lay deep in the streets of Winesburg. It had begun to snow about ten o'clock in the morning and a wind sprang up and blew the snow in clouds along Main Street. The frozen mud roads that led into town were fairly smooth and in places ice covered the mud.

"There will be good sleighing," said Will Henderson, standing by the bar in Ed Griffith's saloon. Out of the saloon he went and met Sylvester West the druggist stumbling along in the kind of heavy overshoes called arctics. "Snow will bring the people into town on Saturday," said the druggist. The two men stopped

and discussed their affairs. Will Henderson, who had
on a light overcoat and no overshoes, kicked the heel
of his left foot with the toe of the right. "Snow will be
good for the wheat," observed the druggest sagely...

A sense of place. From this one excerpt we know a number
of things: the time of year (snow on the ground), a small town
location (Main Street, mud roads leading to town), rural area
(wheat-growing country), quiet atmosphere (major saloon)...
It's a setting we can picture in our minds, one with simple vir-
tues and simple truth. What would be more natural than for
two citizens to meet in casual conversation along the street,
discuss the weather with some gravity and explore its consequences (while one kicks the heel of one shoe with the toe of
another)? One imagines the snow will make good sleighing,
the other offers it as a boon to wheat growing.

This sense of place puts us right into the story, and when
Anderson develops his chapter further we see that it will be
about a teacher in the town of Winesburg, Ohio. But now we
also know what will be behind the little circumstances that
make up the story—the character and the personality of the
town. If the writer is able to understand and portray fully his
or her own sense of place, the reader has to nod with
assurance. "I know where we are, it feels right."

What we are dealing with here is the entire environment of
a story, not only its general background or broad sweep. We
can write about the mountains or the snow on the street or
the cold, brisk air, but to effectively harness a sense of place
we have to get specific. As Helen Haukeness suggests, we
have to write about "...furniture, weather, people, tools,
toys, clutter, lighting, odors..."

The things that make it memorable.

The prison smell assaulted him from the first moment, vaguely sour, distinctly penetrating, reminding him of a man's room that had not been well cleaned. The sharp corridor lights and harsh human noises made him wonder if anyone could retain a sense of comfort here...

Our focus has shifted to the narrowest point. We examine individual traits and circumstances because this will give us clues to where we are. A writer must be concerned about these specific concerns because it is a mosaic we are trying to create—a full, complete picture out of various interconnected parts.

A sense of place is our tool with which to do it.

Watch how Larry McMurtry provides the reader with an unforgettable scene portrayal in his novel, *Texasville*. Here we have the Thalia, Texas Centennial Committee meeting to plan the big pageant. Duane, the story's protagonist, is the chairman of the committee, and the subject of hiring a consultant has come up. Note how McMurtry uses local accents and local characterization to get across the idea of the type of town Thalia represents and what its aspirations are in connection with the centennial celebration:

"I have the name of a man from Brooklyn who directs pageants," Duane said. "He did one down in Throckmorton County and they were real pleased with him."

"Is Brooklyn over near Tyler, or where would it be at?" the Reverend Rawley inquired.

"It's part of New York City," Duane informed him. "He comes with a crew of three, to help him with special effects. We're gonna need a little light show when we're doing the Creation."

"The Lord didn't employ electricity," G.G.

pointed out. He saw it as his duty to fend off any skits that might lead to a liberal interpretation of the Bible.

"He employed lightning," Sonny said. "That's electricity."

"He didn't employ nobody from Brooklyn, New York," G.G. said. "The man might be a Catholic."

Duane sighed. "He's supposed to be real good with fight scenes," he said. "We're doing about ten wars, we need somebody who knows how to stage fight scenes."

"Most people around here already know how to fight," G.G. said...

The characterizations are sharply drawn here, we can imagine the fundamentalist preacher rising indignantly to preserve the pure name of the Lord, we can picture Duane, his patience tried but his determination unflagged. The scene represents a portrayal of small-town politics and small-town prejudices played out in that time-worn setting, the local committee. We don't need to read about the dusty landscape or the boiling summer weather or the tenuous oil-drilling economy to understand the author's sense of place...

We get it from a literal-minded preacher whose world reaches about as far as he can see and whose speech identifies his level of education and tolerance; we get it from a group of citizens who believe their small town is important enough to celebrate a one hundreth birthday and who consider the story of Creation, as well as the replay of every United States war, to be of equal significance as the birth of the town; we get it from Duane whose feelings for his town are stronger than he would like to admit.

A sense of place—a small Texas town preparing for a centennial celebration. The author has been there, and he wants us to feel it with him.

In our modern world, sometimes we need to reach out for a more dramatic reference than a familiar characterization in order to grasp our sense of place. Sometimes we need to utilize mass culture to give us an identity with our readers; sometimes we need to refer to items we have in common. Louise Erdrich, the novelist, believes we are tied to one another through "... the brand names of objects, to symbols like the golden arches, to stories of folk heroes like Ted Turner and Colonel Sanders, to entrepreneurs of comforts that cater to our mobility like Conrad Hilton..."

In short, she thinks that when we use such signs of modern living with our writing, we give our readers a "context" in which to follow the story. It is a lively, thoroughly familiar picture frame that now projects the story.

Is she right?

Here's a story from John Sayles, the writer and film director. In *Children of the Silver Screen,* see if Sayles's reference to mass culture items give the story greater dimension, more drama. Shine manages a small movie theatre, and on this his last day, he is showing a Humphrey Bogart film, "The Treasure of Sierra Madre". His successor has arrived, and it's obvious the theatre is going X-rated. Shine now readies himself to collect tickets for his last show:

They blew in, the Jujyfruits and Almond Joys, Junior Mints and Planters nuts, they grin and wince into bad Bogart impressions, they match wits naming the Magnificent Seven, or the Seven Dwarfs, or even the seven major Golden Age studios. Dopey, they say, Warners and Universal. Steve McQueen and Charles Bronson, they say. Grumpy. A boy who looks like the Spirit of Che Guevara does a soggy soft-shoe in front of the men's room door. The fat girl in the poncho tumbles for a box of popcorn, large, with a nickel's extra butter. A boy in a cape and a girl with a yellow slicker do a brief exchange from a Marx Brothers picture...

Here, then, are the trappings of our mass culture, from familiar movies and familiar characters in those movies to familiar things to eat and familiar people doing the eating. It is the lobby of the theatre just before the doors open, and don't we get a sense of place? Haven't we been here before, somewhere, sometime?

Try and read this passage without brand names, without the movie and movie-character names. Substitute unfamiliar words... does it seem the same? Is the sense of place comfortable, certain?

Probably not.

That's the key. We want to develop our sense of place, and so we must consider a variety of items, from earliest memories to those which are the most familiar trappings of our mass culture.

We must think scenery, structures, streets, speech patterns, the amenities of life, the entire environment...

But it's also important to think brand names, symbols, folk heroes, paranoias, failures...

Then we have our sense of place and the story can proceed.

2

How Many Details?

I read once that the most effective manner to portray setting is to think of myself as a television camera. I would be portable, recordable and focus-changeable. That is, I could fasten on a scene at one angle, and then I could change that angle by the twist of a dial so the scene could be narrowed or widened, closed in or made more remote. The author, finding this imagery appealing, went on to advise me that television camerawork often begins with a wide-angle long shot and then zooms to a close-up in the interest of establishing location and scene.

I remember the author asking... why can't books be written the same way? Why can't we start our setting from a broad perspective and work to a narrow focus? Why can't we begin with a forest and portray a single tree? Or an ocean and a single ship? Or a city and a single street?

The answer is sometimes we can—and do—work things this way. But we don't *have* to, and that's what makes story writing so challenging. We have choices.

Note what happens when the camera begins with a wide angled lens: there are myriad items that seep into our consciousness, regardless of their relevance to the story; if it's a landscape, we see earth and sky, ground contour and growing things, humans and/or animals, vague and fuzzy details that form a part of the broad scene. As the camera moves in, some details take on distinct form, and now we start to feel a sense of where we are because the details themselves grasp us with recognition. We see faces and houses, we hear noises, we feel heat.

But we don't have to start with such a wide-angled lens. Couldn't we begin a story this way?

> From a little after two o'clock until almost sundown of the long still hot weary dead September afternoon they sat in what Miss Coldfield still called the office because her father had called it that—a dim hot airless room with the blinds all closed and fastened for forty-three summers because when she was a girl someone had believed that light and moving air carried heat and that dark was always cooler...

This is the opening of William Faulker's *Absalom, Absalom*. Note that Faulkner doesn't begin with a description of the south, or Mississippi or even the town where the action will develop. We are in the office in the heat of the day, and there is tradition and history in what is about to unfold. Faulkner doesn't use a wide-angled lens, he concentrates on what is happening in that room, and we don't need to be brought into the story by proceeding from some broader perspective. We start with the specific.

What about this opening?

His face had the look of dark certainty, but we knew it was a convenient mask. His voice betrayed him as he whispered about the barricades of fire that ringed the cave entrance...

Or this?

The phone rang again, and now he heard it. Shrill destroyer of comfortable sleep, cottony awareness.

"Mayor!" an angry voice,

"Huh?" Mettalic mouth taste.

A hushed sob through the earpiece."... police... my son... no reason..."

In either example we have a few details that set out what we need to know to understand where we are. Human emotion portrayed so that where it takes place is evident... in a cave or in a mayor's bedroom. Specific locations with narrow focus.

The idea of using a lot of detail with any description goes back at least as far as Daniel Defoe in the eighteenth century. For Defoe a mass of descriptive detail was a way of adding authenticity to his story, a way of making it more plausible. He came to believe that a relationship between setting and the action was possible, that by including many physical details the story itself could move forward.

Is he right? Here's a passage from Defoe's *Robinson Crusoe,* with the narrator describing how he built a canoe to take him from his shipwreck-island:

I felled a cedar tree, and I question much whether Solomon ever had such a one for the building of the Temple at Jerusalem; it was five feet ten inches in diameter at the lower part next to the stump, and four feet eleven inches diameter at the end of twenty two feet, where it lessened and then parted into branches.

It was not without infinite labor that I felled this tree;
I was twenty days hacking and hewing at the bottom,
and fourteen more getting the branches and limbs,
and the vast spreading head of it, cut off...

Don't we get caught up in his effort, in his obsession to survive? Each detail presents us with a quandary—will he overcome it or won't he? Then, as he makes his way, the details themselves become steps along his path to ultimate rescue. He survives, he continues to survive, and we, the readers, share his burdens and his triumphs.

In this sense, then, the mass of details do interact with the plot of the story because the details are, themselves, the story. They make the story.

Substantial detail can still work today, though we must be careful about how we use it. Look to some of the work of Irving Wallace or Arthur Hailey, for example. These authors go to great lengths to present substantial information while weaving all those details through the story.

That, of course, is the key. A strong story where the details, no matter how numerous, are necessary. Could we ever doubt that the details in *Robinson Crusoe* were absolutely essential to the story? If we didn't have those details, what kind of story would we have?

A boring narrative, I suggest, without much tension or excitement.

But be careful when using great amounts of detail. As Robie MacCauley and George Lanning suggest, "Excessive detail, like that which is merely picturesque, proves only that the writer has been busy about his homework." The details must mean something to the story, they must do something *for* the story. Try this: read over some prose with lengthy descriptions, then read it over without the descriptions. Is something missing? Does it read more dramatically with or without the descriptions?

If it can stand without the lengthy descriptions, guess what?

The author overwrote.

One area where there is a tendency to use too much detail is in stories where the writer has no way of knowing the true facts—science fiction, particularly, but also stories that occurred in the far past. We can research some of these items, to be sure, but research takes us only so far, and at some point we have to rely on our imaginations and story-telling talents. The problem is that in attempting to create a realistic setting, we offer so many facts to buttress that make-believe world we are creating. We strive for authenticity, just as Defoe did with *Robinson Crusoe*. But it really isn't necessary. One author advises that the important details, no matter the kind of story we write, involve specific colors, shapes and textures. These, he feels, are the keys.

No question he has a point. Consider the following passage from Ray Bradbury's *Martial Chronicles*. In this opening Bradbury doesn't try to paint an exotic scene; it isn't necessary to make it seem so unusual just because the setting happens to be Mars. He limits his details, and the story might be taking place next door:

It was quiet in the deep morning of Mars, as quiet as a cool black well, with stars shining in the canal waters, and, breathing in every room, the children curled with their spiders in closed hands...

Doesn't he capture our interest because this is a setting with which we could easily become familiar? He mentions colors (black), shapes (waters, canal, curled) and textures (quiet, cool, shining), and this gives us a well-defined flavor of where the story takes place and how matters will proceed.

Just a few well-placed details so we feel comfortable with the story.

The big question remains, though... out of the mass of details where colors, shapes and textures proliferate, what choices should we make? What details are the best ones?

The most effective approach is to imagine ourselves in the scene: it is we who do the looking and the absorbing, and we know what will strike us most forcefully. We seek "key details" with this method, ever mindful that use of detail can overrun us if we aren't careful. No two writers deal with it exactly the same, but there is underlying similiarity among the works of accomplished professionals. See, for example, how these novelists handle it:

"... to 'be there' is a tremendous help in [telling my story]. It enables me to pare down descriptive passages to the very minimum, because all I have to do is describe the few key features in any particular room or garden or landscape that strike me the most, just as if I were really there..."—*G. Masterton*

"The most vivid 'atmospheric' setting is done, not with elaborate description which tires the reader's powers of mental build-up, but with the selection of one or two telling details..."—*Mary Stewart*

A few key features, one or two telling details, these are what it takes. Shapes, colors, textures, these are what to choose. Details that matter, details that encourage the plot to move forward without, at the same time, distracting the reader's attention.

See how Graham Greene, an acknowledged master of underplayed detail, does it in his story, *Cheap in August*. Mary Watson, an English woman married to an American professor, is on a summer vacation in Jamaica because her husband is off researching in Europe. She is staying in a large commercial hotel which caters to tour groups, mostly American tour groups, and she is appalled by some of her fellow female guests. Note how each detail adds to the story yet also provides us with a vivid picture of the scene. Note, too, how few details there really are:

> Huge buttocks were exposed in their full horror in tight large-patterned Bermuda shorts. Heads were bound in scarves to cover rollers which were not removed even by lunchtime—they stuck out like small mole-hills. Daily she watched the bums lurch by like hippos on the way to the water. Only in the evening would the women change from the monstrous shorts into monstrous cotton frocks, covered with mauve or scarlet flowers in order to take dinner on the terrace where formality was demanded in the book of rules...

Don't we get a clear picture of these women, can't we imagine ourselves in a quiet chair watching them? Doesn't this paint a vivid scene, one of tastelessness and over-indulgence? Mary Watson's lack of empathy for her fellow guests is the crux of this story, so Greene's portrayal of her offended sensibilities through physical description works perfectly.

But see how he does it... through what they wear in color and shape. That's all. We don't see the women talk, we have no idea what their faces look like, we don't even know their names. All we know is how they fill their clothes.

A few key features, one or two telling details.

Do we really need more?

3

The Value of an Imperfect Memory

Most of us can remember our first date, at what age it occurred, the person we went with. It was an important event in
our young lives, and as the years have moved along, its importance hasn't really diminished. It represented a classic step
into young adulthood, the beginning of a long passage that
has taken us to where we are today.

Important time, important memory.

But how many of us remember what we wore on that date,
whether we really wished we were somewhere else, the month
it happened and what we told our friends about it?

In short, do we have total recall?

Suppose we wanted to do a story, and we wanted to weave
in a first-date scene... suppose further we had a clear memory
of our own first date, and it seemed a good sequence to use in
this story. The question then becomes...

Do we wish to *reproduce* the experience?

or

Do we wish to *recreate* it?

Reproducing the experience means we act as a camera, picking out each detail and laying it before the viewer *exactly as it appears to be.*

Recreating the experience means we act as a painter, picking out details but ennobling them with a character and a style that suits the painter and not the truthfulness of the scene.

One is reproduction, the other is creation.

One gives us facts, the other gives us art.

The key is in our memories and what we use of them to form a piece of writing. We can, of course, jot down *everything,* missing no detail or circumstance. We can reproduce the event just as it happened... and wonder why it doesn't sing with drama as our memories tell us it should.

I missed nothing, we reassure ourselves. *It happened just this way... didn't it?*

Yes, yes, we answer. Every detail remembered.

But it's not art. It's not creation and it's not fiction. For that to happen we must find drama, and we must use our inventive skills. A story doesn't work just because it happened. Writers know this intuitively, and they also know that a story's freshness is dependent upon the ability to create drama out of unreconstructed facts.

Remembering facts is one thing... but remembering them and then turning them into a good story is something else. "Remote memories, already distorted by the imagination, are most useful for the purposes of scene," said Elizabeth Bowen many years ago. "Unfamiliar or *once-seen* places yield more than do familiar, often-seen places." The more we come to know a place, the more we see it, the more confined we are by what we have seen or felt. We become prisoners of our own knowledge, and that level of familiarity makes it difficult if not impossible for us to develop anything that is not factually correct.

And as we know, facts don't make a story. Drama does.

An imperfect memory, then, is not a burden to the writer. It is a boon companion in the same way as a reading experience is... they both teach us to think in story terms, to create. Here's Arturo Vivante on the subject of memory:

> What is memory? Why do we remember? We remember where our house is so we can find it and go back to it. We remember what happened to us in a certain situation so that we may avoid or seek again that sort of situation. We remember someone who has died and whom we loved, because it is the thing that will come closest to reviving that person for us... that is why we remember—to renew the past, and not, primarily, to recount it...

To *renew* the past, not to *recount* it!

Now, when we write about our first date, we think about those things that made it memorable: what he/she looked like, what pressures or uncertainties existed, whether we ever went out with that person again, what, if anything, happened. We renew the memory, and then we turn it in to a story, changing facts and circumstances to provide tension, a defined plot and a workable setting. It doesn't matter if we can't remember where we went on that first date—make it up! It doesn't matter if we can't remember who else was there, or we can't remember why we went out with that particular person—make it up!

The fact that we had a first date is the memory we want to

renew; what we do with that memory is what distinguishes the fiction writer from the reporter.

Eudora Welty has written a wide variety of fiction, much of it set in the south. In *The Optimist's Daughter* she has a major scene set in rural West Virginia with two characters, a mother and daughter, stepping off the train in the early morning. They stand on a steep rock:

> ... all of the world that they could see in the mist being their rock and its own iron bell on a post with its rope hanging down. Her mother gave the rope a pull and at its sound, almost at the moment of it, large and close to them appeared a gray boat with two of the boys at the oars. At their very feet had been a river. The boat came breasting out of the mist, and in they stepped. All new things in life were meant to come like that.
>
> Bird dogs went streaking the upslanted pasture through the sweet long grass that swept them as high as their noses. While it was still day on top of the mountain, the light still warm on the cheek, the valley was dyed blue under them...

An ethereal setting to be sure! This is the young daughter's first glimpse of the West Virginia that part of her family settled. We can't tell from the words alone whether Eudora Welty is relying on her memory or her imagination, though the description is vivid enough either way. It would be hard to believe that at some point in her life she hadn't experienced the scene she offers...

And, in fact, she had. In an interview a few years ago she had this exchange with her questioner:

Welty: My mother came from West Virginia...
                  [*The Optimist's Daughter*] was literal

Interv: memory, up on the mountain and the
             sights and sounds up there.
             I've always been curious as to how West
             Virginia got in that novel so strongly.
Welty: Well, we spent every summer visiting the
             families. My father was from Ohio and
             we went to his father's farm down in
             southern Ohio, and to the home on the
             mountaintop in West Virginia. That's
             where all my kinfolks were...

So she was writing from memory, but note it is a selective
memory. She doesn't tell us she remembers everything about
that mountaintop in West Virginia, only that she was there
and that is was familiar country. After a lot of years there
had to be things that escaped her recollection, and she
doesn't try to recover them.

We're served only those items which provide a dramatic
base for the setting, those which touch our senses and give us
a feeling of "being there."

But suppose the writer's memory isn't sufficient for the
scene she wants to write, suppose the recollection of what
happened doesn't fit the scene?

What then?

Eudora Welty again. In *Delta Wedding* it is 1923 and she
has a young girl from the midwest visit her mother's family in
the delta country of Mississippi. It is the girl's first visit, and
she will stay seven days—the entire length of the book. It is a
story with a number of characters, most of them family, all
interacting with the wedding as the focal point. See how Welty sets a family scene through Dabney, the bride-to-be:

It was next afternoon. Dabney came down the
stairs vaguely in time to the song Mary Lamar

43

Mackey was rippling out in the music room—"Drink to Me Only With Thine Eyes." "Oh, I'm a wreck," she sighed absently.

"Did you have your breakfast? Then run on to your aunts," said her mother, pausing in the hall below, pointing a silver dinner knife at her. "You're a girl engaged to be married and your aunts want to see you." "Your aunts" always referred to the two old-maid sisters of her father's who lived at the Grove, the old place on the river, Aunt Primrose and Aunt Jim Allen, and not to Aunt Tempe who had married Uncle Pinck, or Aunt Rowena or Aunt Annie Laurie who were dead...

We know the book will take in a lot of characters, and the question for us is whether Eudora Welty is relying on her memory to set these scenes or whether she is creating them from her imagination. Is this *her* family she is writing about, the family of someone she knows well, or is it total fiction?

Once again we turn to that same interview a few years back. The interviewer offers a comment:

Interv: So you never had the experience that many southern children have of being 'trapped' in a room where all the relatives are talking and telling family stories.

Welty: I've experienced that but only as a treat, you know, in the summer. I had to make all that up for *Delta Wedding*...

The scenes in the book where the family members are vividly interacting come in part from her imagination and in part from her memory. But neither, standing alone, would have been sufficient for the book she wanted to write. She had to go back to her memory for what the characters might have said to one another, but she had to put it all into a new setting, and she had to be creative about putting it all together.

I had to make all that up...

Her memory gave her the key, but her sense of creativity opened the door. See the difference in the way she approached the two books: in *The Optimist's Daughter* she uses her memory to zero in on the action and setting, but in *Delta Wedding* she conjures a new setting and partially fictitious action. Her memory is less effective for one than the other, but in either case she doesn't get trapped into total recall. She remembers, but she doesn't recount.

As writers, we don't want to remember too much because, in the words of Peter Stillman, "... near-total recall would be a cruel handicap. You cannot write imaginatively about past moments if you remember them too clearly. Their details become too burdensome, and hence their essences escape."

That is the value of an imperfect memory. The opportunity it gives us to enlarge upon our recollections, and the challenge it offers to turn out a story other people will want to read.

Make that scene!... and imagine, imagine, imagine!

4

How Much Research?

Years ago I wanted to write a novel set in the coal mining regions of Pennsylvania. I had a general familiarity with the area but that would not be sufficient.

I plunged into it with excitement becaue I *knew* what I was looking for—I wanted to re-create a town's moral disintegration and set it within a political-social conflict. It would be John O'Hara updated.

Oh, how I researched. Weeks and weeks at the library, careful notes inscribed on a mound of index cards, letters to faraway sources, telephone calls and personal interviews. No one would know his setting better, no one could be more prepared.

After almost six months I was ready to write. No loose ends remained in the research, and I had so many things to tell. Confidence coursed through me.

The writing sped along, and my treasure house of information translated easily to the written page. I had no doubt the reader would experience in vivid fashion the way it was in a Pennsylvania coal-mining town. From the proper construction of a coal sluice to a history of coal-mining extraction techniques to the training procedures of nineteenth century coal miners, the reader would understand and empathize.

When the novel was finished, I presented it to an editor friend for comment.

"It probably needs one more draft," I said. "But I'm pleased so far."

"Coal mining town," he said. "Hasn't that been done?"

"Not like this."

A couple of weeks later we met, and he returned the manuscript. "I've read it." he said.

"I have some changes—they'll refine it some."

He shook his head slowly. "Best advice I can give you—start again. This won't get published."

"The plot's weak," I said. "It needs more story."

He shook his head again. "Start over."

"The characters must be dull."

He tapped the pile of white manuscript pages. "The problem isn't just one thing. It's your approach. What you've done is to tell me more about a Pennsylvania coal-mining town than I want to know. Facts instead of a story. With some changes this might make a pretty good textbook..."

Which was something I certainly didn't want to hear.

My problem? I fell in love with my research, and I couldn't imagine the reader not enjoying the information I found. So I told—everything.

The peculiar circumstances of developing a workable setting mean we have to deal, for the most part, with physical environment. We have to describe *things* (such as a properly constructed coal sluice), and the risk we run is that we offer too many details, so the story will suffer.

We want our setting to be realistic, but that doesn't mean that the more facts we present, the more realistic it will be. It isn't a case of some being good and more being better. We have to choose and choose carefully, something I didn't do with my ill-fated novel. That doesn't mean, however, that we shouldn't do extensive research. The research is the foundation for whatever comes later, but for the writer the key is this:

—Use enough information so the reader understands and is not overwhelmed by the setting; *make it a judicious sprinkling.*

See how Michael Crichton does it with his novel, *Congo,* about an expedition for diamond exploration in Africa. The team of explorers, led by mathematician Karen Ross, would use the latest technology in their quest. Here, the author explains where the search would be conducted and then has Ross add some further information:

On a map the Great Rift depression was marked by two features: a series of thin vertical lakes—Malawi, Tanganyika, Kivu, Mobutu—and a series of volcanoes, including the only active volcanoes in Africa at Virunga. These volcanoes in the Virunga chain were active: Mukenko, Mubuti, and Kanagarawi. They rose 11000-15000 feet above the Rift Valley to the east, and the Congo Basin to the west. Thus Virunga seemed a good place to look for diamonds. Her next step was to investigate the ground truth.

"What's ground truth?" Peter asked.

"At ERTS we deal mostly in remote sensing," she explained. "Satellite photographs, aerial run-bys, radar side scans. We carry millions of remote images, but there's no subsitute for ground truth, the experience of a team actually on site, finding out what's there..."

Lots of details and unfamiliar names and designations here, undoubtedly the product of substantial research. The geological descriptions in the first paragraph give a scientific explanation to why the search would be concentrated there, but they are neither so lengthy nor so esoteric as to numb the reader. What a few selected facts of setting will do is provide authenticity for the action to follow; it will provide an appropriate background.

And this is what Crichton does. His research must have uncovered much more than what he puts on the page, but then he wasn't interested in offering a lesson in geography. What he wanted to do—and succeeded in doing—was to sprinkle enough facts to keep the story going because the Rift Valley, of course, is where the search for the diamonds will concentrate.

Then note Ross's speech. A brief survey of the high-tech designation "ground truth," but here again the details are kept to a minimum, mostly in the form of examples. (Why examples? Because they tend to create images in the reader's mind, and these are both more dramatic and more memorable than simple exposition.) To uncover the essence of "ground truth," Crichton must have had to do additional research, but he gives us just enough so we understand without having to wade through a high-tech operating manual.

How much research we do, then, is dependent more on

how we want that research to move the story than on insuring the reader understands *everything*. What we as writers may find out through research is one thing; what we should offer to the reader of what we find out is something else.

Just a sprinkling of facts is best.

Suppose we want to write about a world that none of us has ever lived in—it could be in the past or it could be in the future. We know we'll have to research, and the acute question is what should we seek to learn? Historical novelist G. Masterton has some definite ideas: "I undertake an enormous amount of research that I never use; in fact I use as *little* of my historical research as possible... All I want to be able to do is convey my historical world with the confidence of somebody who happens to know what kind of calendar might be hanging on the wall. What kind of boots that old man sitting in the corner might be wearing, and how much he paid for them."

I undertake an enormous amount of research that I never use... The talents of the writer are directed towards fact gathering, not to be disgorged at the reader but to be picked over and reformed into dramatic prose. Could one suppose that Masterton would uncover the type of calendar on the wall without also uncovering the kind of furniture in the room, the makeup of the house, the size of the floors, the height of the ceiling...?

But he may choose only to describe the calendar because that is sufficient to provide the appropriate dramatic effect.

In the same way, novelist Richard Condon presents the products of *his* research in *A Trembling Upon Rome,* the story of the schism in the Catholic Church during the latter fourteenth and early fifteenth centuries. The Church has two Popes, one sitting in Rome, the other in Avignon, and Condon's story is a dramatization of the split. Major characters appearing in the book include high church, political and military officials. In this passage he shows the corruption that was present in Avignon by listing the prices for church favors.

There was a graduated scale of prices that permitted the laity to choose their confessor outside their regular parish. The pope could change either canon law or divine law; but the divine law was changed only if there was enough money; money could buy anything, deliver any matter of permission to the petitioner.

For a king to carry his sword on Christmas Day—150 groschen

To legitimatize illegitimate children—60 groschen

For giving a converted Jew permission to visit his parents—40 percent

To free a bishop from an archbishop—30 groschen

To divide a dead man and put him into two graves—30 groschen

To permit a nun to have two maids—20 groschen

To obtain immunity from excommunication—6 groschen

To receive stolen goods to the value of 1000 groschen—50 groschen

Does this information help us understand the level of morality in Avignon in the fifteenth century? Do we need to know much more about how the church controlled the lives of the people and what were the important concerns? Does this set the scene for a story of high-level political-sexual-military high jinx?

Condon does give us physical description at other points in

the book so we can form a mental image of fifteenth-century Avignon. But his research, undoubtedly, uncovered many more facts than he has placed in the book, and when he wanted to give us a portrayal of the relationship between the church and the people, he doesn't describe beautiful cathedrals, penitent worshipping or high-holy-day processions...

He gives us a laundry list of favors that can be bought.

Doesn't that put things in dramatic perspective?

As we research we will come upon a lot of information that will bear upon our subject but will not interest us. Facts and circumstances—statistics, for example, or tables or overly complicated explanations—that we'll tend to put to one side or to ignore altogether. They don't seem to fit into a scene-setting arrangement.

Here's where we should be careful because it's just such items that might give an undeniable ring of authenticity to our setting. For example, it would have been easy to understand Richard Condon passing by the laundry list of church favors in order to concentrate on more seemingly dramatic facts to illuminate the moral state of fifteenth-century Avignon. A church trial, for instance, or major speech by the pope or an archbishop.. something that could readily catch attention.

But he chose the laundry list. And it worked!

"Not every last bit of essential research is interesting,' says novelist Lawrence Block. "There are things you have to know, matters of fact that will trip you up if you get them demonstrably wrong." He's right. It may not interest us to learn the mating habits of an insect the size of our fingernail, but if our story turns on the bite of that insect then we'd better learn all we can about it. In the same way, our research may turn up facts about how an old building was constructed—materials, dimensions, style and so forth. If that building figures in the story in more than a passing manner, we had better come to grips with those construction facts, even though we think of blueprints as a foreign language. The one thing we don't want to do is make an assumption about the physical characteristics of a setting just because we find the basic facts too uninteresting to pursue.

Nothing will push egg on our faces any quicker than to be caught short by a reader who knows we didn't do our homework... "an oversight"... "overlooked"... "didn't seem important"... might mollify the sharp-eyed reader, but as writers we should have taken the all-important next step and checked it out!

The final goal of research may be to sprinkle facts on our setting, but we've got to be sure they are the *right* facts. We know when that is because what's interesting and what's not is the question we reserve for the reader, not for our research.

"This could make a good textbook eventually," said my editor friend years ago.

I wrote it as a novel, I wanted to say. Instead, I swallowed and gathered up the manuscript pages. "Start over, you think?"

"Afraid so."

The research had been fun, anyway.

5

Setting As a Major Character

Here's a real-live note from an editor to a writer:
...[Y]ou use your setting to affect your characters as well as influence them. And, in a broader sense, your setting is Government, and you, like Cozzens and a few other contemporary novelists, know how much a great institution becomes a part of the people connected with it...

Comments that are admiring, supportive, instructive... a large pat on the back for making his setting more than simple background. The writer gives his setting importance, and this has undeniable consequences for the story.

The book in question is *Advise and Consent,* the writer is Allen Drury and the editor is William Sloane. The comments were offered in August, 1960, and Sloane's words presaged a torrent of praise and success for the book which dealt with political maneuvering and scandal at the highest Washington levels.

What Sloane picks out as especially praiseworthy is how Drury develops his setting—government—so that it becomes an important character in the story. Not merely something that influences others to act (as we'll see in the next chapter), but as a force in and of itself. Sloane, himself, calls such techniques "not using scenery for its own sake," but "central parts of the stories their writers laid in them."

The point is simply this: a setting can be powerful enough to affect how every character in the story acts and reacts with every other character, how every event is determined. Is there any doubt, for example, that the sanitarium in Thomas Mann's *The Magic Mountain* is the guiding force in the story, that without it, the story, itself, would have little meaning? The sanitarium—the setting—plays a major role in the story because all who live and die within it are pushed along by what it means. People come to the Magic Mountain for relief and survival, and they find a world completely encapsulated, unentangled with what they used to know. The sanitarium *is* their world now, and everything they do is the consequence of that.

Why would a writer want to make his or her setting do more than routine background work in a story? It is, after all, an added burden in that characters must not only interact with each other but now they must also have a continuing relationship with the setting. If the setting is the sanitarium, as in *The Magic Mountain,* the characters must think and feel and act with reference at all times to the fact they are in a well-defined encapsulated world. For some writers this could bring stagnation because story movement would be resricted; for other writers it might bring frustration because they want different characters to acquire more importance.

Why, then, would a writer build up a setting and make it so important? Two reasons come immediately to mind: first, a setting with major significance offers a constant in the story, something the writer can always turn to when he or she wants to move the story in a different direction, perhaps even as a change of pace. The setting's significance doesn't vary. It will affect the other characters and the story, too, and it will do so in predictable ways (at least as far as the writer is concerned); second, the setting having major importance becomes a self-limiting factor for the writer; the story will never progress beyond the limits of the setting because the setting is too important to transcend. In other words, once the writer creates his important setting, whether it is government or a sanitarium high in the Swiss Alps or any other creation, he works within it, and this has the benefit of allowing the writer to control his story, to keep things tight. Think of doing somersaults on a gym mat... everything is firm, yet comfortable, so long as we stay on the mat... but suppose we whirl off the mat... we're no longer on familiar territory, and the results could be disastrous. The mat is our setting, and it is important enough to be crucial for our success.

Now suppose we wish to develop our setting so it is a major character in our story—what must we do? More than fifty years ago John Frederick offered two simple rules. The writer, he said "...must have a very active sense of place as such, and a conviction of its importance in human affairs."

—an active sense of place

—a conviction of the setting's importance

From chapter one we have a familiarity with a sense of place—the totality of our experiences and understandings about where we were born, grew up and now live. A sense of place in a story we write is important enough when we are developing the background, but when we want to put the setting into a prominent role as a character in the story, our sense of place takes on added significance. Can we imagine *The Magic Mountain* being written if Thomas Mann, himself, did not have first-hand experience with daily life in a high mountain sanitarium? Or could Ernest Hemingway have written a *A Farewell to Arms* if he hadn't been through the war and seen its carnage at first hand? If Hemingway set out to make the war a major character in his novel, he needed to be certain of his place within that setting, and it had to be an active sense of place because the war was too important to the story. That is, the war defined the characters and the plot, and if the war wasn't vividly presented, the characters and the story would sag.

We don't develop strong setting without an active sense of place.

Simple as that.

Nor do we develop a strong setting if we don't believe it is important. We have to believe firmly that our setting should be a major character in the story. The reason? The setting is within touching range of the action and the other characters at all times. It is always there! If we didn't believe it was important, our writing would reflect it. As a major force in the story it would lack substance and commitment; it would have little life.

Should this happen, the entire story could fall apart.

So... when we decide to make our setting more than workable background, we have to be believers in its importance, not only to our story but to the general human condition.

See how E.M. Forster does it with *A Passage to India,* his

fine novel about the days of the British Raj and race discrimination and empire building. The setting — India — is, of course, a major character in the work, and Forster combines a great understanding for the country and the people with an undoubted belief that what he is writing about has great importance. In this scene Miss Quested, the English woman who is engaged to a British army officer, and Aziz, her Indian translator and general aide, are travelling through the sparsely inhabited countryside. They spot an elephant in the distance:

As the elephant moved towards the hills... a new quality occurred, a spiritual silence which invaded more senses than the ear. Life went on as usual, but had no consequences, that is to say, sounds did not echo or thoughts develop. Everything seemed cut off at its root, and therefore affected with illusion. For instance, there were some mounds by the edge of the track, low, serrated, and touched with white-wash. What were these mounds—graves, breasts cf the goddess Pavanti? The villagers beneath gave both replies. Again, there was a confusion about a snake which was never cleared up. Miss Quested saw a thin, dark object reared on end at the farther side of a watercourse, and said "A snake!" The villagers agreed, and Aziz explained: yes, a black cobra, very venemous, who had reared himself up to watch the passing of an elephant...

The exotic nature of the landscape alone (elephants, whitewashed mounds, black cobra snakes) provides a definite sense of place, even if the author goes on to paint it as illusory. The point is it represents more than "furniture" of the locality, it is the product of experiences not only for the villagers but for the narrator and the other characers, as well. No one knows quite what the mounds represent... and there is confusion about the appearance of the object that resembles a black cobra snake. Does not this very confusion portray the contradictions of India, the "sense of place" the writer wants to show us? Could he depict all of this if he didn't feel strongly about his setting, if he didn't believe it important enough to form a backbone for the story?

How do we know the writer thinks his sense of place is important?

When his story would wither to nothingness without the setting.

Can we imagine *A Passage to India* limited to Miss Quested's sea voyage? Or involved only with life on a British garrison?

Of course not.

As a major character in the story our setting must be vivid enough to have an effect on what happens. If our background is nothing but a vague landscape or an uninteresting room or a home without depth or substance, the story will go forward independently of the setting, and little interconnection will be made.

But where the setting is evoked with vividness, as in *A Passage to India,* everything that happens will be affected by it because it has become a major character.

Vividness. What do we mean by it?

Here are the words of an accomplished novelist.

[The writer] should evoke the background vividly enough for the reader, a stranger, to see, hear, smell, touch, taste and, to a certain extent, actually feel he is there. Through every word of this exposition, the author must keep in mind the emotional responses of his characters...

The reader must *feel* the setting, experience it, live it, if possible. That's vividness.

It could be outer space... or the frozen slabs of Antarctica... or the massive inner structure of a huge aircraft carrier... or the jungle...

Anything that could develop excitement, suspense and uncertainty.

Consider the jungle. Couldn't it operate as a major character in a story? See how Joseph Conrad works with it in his classic novella, *Heart of Darkness,* the story of Marlow, a ship captain in Africa, sent to search for Kurtz, an ivory hunter who seems to have disappeared somewhere in the jungle.

Marlow's trek up a treacherous river and his ultimate meeting with Kurtz are developed by the nature of the jungle through which both men survive. Conrad doesn't blast us with flat, lengthy descriptions of the jungle; rather he touches us with hints, inferences and occasional vivid glimpses of what it is like:

"Going up that river was like travelling back to the earliest beginnings of the world, when vegetation rioted on the earth and the big trees were kings. An empty stream, a great silence, an impenetrable forest. The air was warm, thick, heavy, sluggish. There was no joy in the brilliance of sunshine. The long stretches of the waterway ran on, deserted, into the gloom of overshadowed distances. On silvery sandbanks hippos and alligators sunned themselves side by side. The broadening waters flowed through a mob of wooded islands; you lost your way on that river as you would in a desert, and butted all day long against shoals, trying to find the channel, till you thought yourself betwitched and cut off forever from something you had known once—somewhere far away—in another existence perhaps—..."

From time to time Conrad does use other phrases to describe the jungle, once in a while even the title phrase, "heart of darkness"... "the earth seemed unearthly"... "the rest of the world was nowhere..."

But he doesn't attempt a lengthy description of the animals or the flora or the insects or the heavy, muggy heat. Merely an occasional mention is all that's needed, so long as the jungle remains a constant presence and its character retains its vividness. The jungle determines whether Marlow arrives upriver, it determines whether Kurtz is still alive, it determines whether Kurtz and Marlow will meet, it determines, finally, why Kurtz seemed to have disappeared and what he now has become.

The jungle, in short, is a major character in the story. It determines what happens, and it determines to whom it will happen.

Without the jungle there would have been no *Heart of Darkness.*

Simple as that.

6

Setting As an Influence on Character

"Daylight comes, and. . ."

The opening, the beginning of a scene, and we have a brand new setting because the darkness has left. The characters may be situated in the same place, they may not have moved one inch, but the daylight brings a changed awareness of surroundings; things are different now.

What we highlight in this new setting can tell us things about the characters in the scene. It can give us a clue about their emotional make-up, it can aid us in understanding them. For example:

> *Daylight comes,* and the splintered remains of forest bear shocked witness to the battlefield carnage. A single soldier sobbing in the muddy underbrush, his body pressing the earth, scrunching into frightful oblivion.. . .

Or:

Daylight comes, and the sand has grown cold, though it didn't seem that way when they first tried it—how many hours ago? He hears her soft breathing, and he winces at memories of their passionate evening. Quiet beach, moonlight, soft ocean. . . He retrieves his hand from hers and pushes himself to his knees, sensing stiffness and gritty taste. The gray dawn belies the clarity of their beach night . . .

The setting in both these cases develops the emotional state of the characters. . . in the first scene the horror of the battlefield shows us a character who wants only to escape its agony, and he mirrors a burrowing animal in his terror; in the second scene the beach at dawn has none of the romance of the beach at midnight, and the character senses such hardened reality.

Setting should never be approached without an awareness that *where* we are can influence *who* we are. In other words, as we create a scene, we should recognize that our setting might be used to develop one or more characters and that such development can then aid in showing motivation or action. If, for example, we set the story in a barren house where the furniture and the furnishings barely give an air of civility, would it not seem consistent to have a character living in that house who was emotionally barren as well? Would not the coldness of the surroundings provide adequate evidence of the person who lives there?

One way to accomplish this is to paint the habits and the mores of people, and in doing so to develop their human sides. The setting need not be physical description such as a house or a garden or a street or a mountainside; it can be, simply, what they do.

See how Albert Camus does it with his novel, *The Plague*, about wartime Oran, Algeria, and written almost a half century ago. Note how we come to understand the people through their habits and their customs:

> Perhaps the easiest way of making a town's acquaintance is to ascertain how the people in it work, how they love, and how they die. In our little town (is this, one wonders, an effect of the climate?) all this is done on much the same lines, with the same feverish yet casual air. The truth is that everyone is bored and devotes himself to cultivating habits. Our citizens work hard, but solely with the object of getting rich. Their chief interest is in commerce, and their chief aim in life is, as they call it, "doing business." Naturally they don't eschew such simpler pleasures as love-making, sea-bathing, going to the pictures. But, very sensibly, they reserve these pastimes for Saturday afternoons and Sundays and employ the rest of the week in making money, as much as possible. In the evening, on leaving the office, they foregather, at an hour that never varies, in the cafés, stroll the same boulevard, or take the air on their balconies. . .

This is the way the people are, and Camus provides us a setting by means of their habits. If they are business oriented, perhaps overly so, doesn't it show us that their characters have to be influenced by this fact, and that what they do and what they say and what they feel will be motivated accordingly? If the citizen's prime goal is to get rich, what place is there for altruism, for spiritual grace and for impracticality?

None, really. Hard-headed realism, profit orientation and wealth accumulation are the personal ethic, and we know this because Camus, the author, tells us it is also the public ethic.

Setting as created by habits and mores.

We can do it, too. If we depict a town by describing its citizens as suspicious and unfriendly, doesn't that aid the reader in picking out character?. . . Or an office where the employees like to play practical jokes on one another—isn't it easy to imagine what kind of person would find this irresistible?. . . Or a college classroom where the students regularly interrupt one another—doesn't this tell something about the professor?

The setting, in other words, need not be physical.

It hasn't always been this way. Two hundred years ago the major purpose of setting was to illustrate action and to make the character vividly evident to the eye. The brighter the setting could be painted, the more it would influence the character and the more the character would stand out for the reader to appreciate. Even today such a technique is not unused—we can see it in the novels of Judith Krantz and Sidney Sheldon, the settings exotic enough so the characters grow more exciting, more interesting. It is the physical descriptions that develop all of this, and these must be vivid indeed!

> Amid the oozing fatness and warm ferments of Froom Vale, at a season when the rush of juices could almost be heard below the hiss of fertilization, it was impossible that the most fanciful love should not grow passionate. The ready hearts existing there were impregnated by their surroundings. . .

This is from *Tess of the D'Urbervilles* by Thomas Hardy, written a long time ago. The passion in these words is almost palpable, isn't it? The setting is so fecund that the characters could not possibly be indifferent, and in fact the setting will develop a motivation for the characters; a burgeoning intensi-

ty in the surroundings will force a growing passion in them.
Vividness, all right.

Joseph Conrad does the same thing in a story called *The Brute*. Note how physical characteristics can portray certain aspects of character:

> On the other side of the fire, imposingly calm and large, sat Mr. Stonor, jammed tight into a capacious Windsor dining chair. There was nothing small about him but his short, white side-whiskers. Yards and yards of extra superfine blue cloth (made up into an overcoat) reposed on a chair by his side. And he must have brought some liner from the sea, because another chair was smothered under his black waterproof, ample as a pull, and made of three-fold oiled silk, double-stitched throughout. A man's hand-bag of the usual size looked like a child's toy on the floor near his feet. . .

Vivid description, once again, only this time it isn't the surroundings, it is the character, himself. His physical proportions will (or can) provide a clue to what he feels and what he does, and we don't need to look to the landscape or nearby objects to develop such an influence. If he's huge, then he'll act as a huge man does, and the setting for the story can be this out-sized human proportion. It can work in reverse, too. A tiny man will also be influenced by his size, and we can be pretty sure he will act and speak in certain ways because of it.

The point is that if we are going to use physical proportion to prod a character along, make sure it is *vivid* physical proportion. Look at Conrad's phrasing:

— imposingly calm and large. . .
— jammed tight.
— nothing small about him. . .

- Yards and yards of extra superfine blue
  cloth. . .
- chair was smothered. . .
- looked like a child's toy. . .
  Vivid, all right.

Today, though, portraying a vivid setting isn't really necessary to show that there can be an influence on the characters. All we need is that the setting is clear enough to understand. The heavens don't have to shake, the landscape doesn't have to erupt, the people don't have to be eight feet tall.

For example:

It was a calm day with a westerly wind fluttering over the tops of the apple trees. The orchard floor was lightly sprinkled with early "drops," those quick-to-mature apples which outgrow their meager stem and don't wait for the picker's choice. . .

Nothing outsized here, nothing painted in stark, bold colors, simply a rural scene at the beginning of apple-picking season. It could influence a host of characters because of its serenity and ruralness, it can motivate behavior consistent with this.

See how Katherine Anne Porter handles a rural scene, and how her setting influences her characters. In her story, *Rope*, a husband and wife move to the country and buy a farmhouse:

On the third day after they moved to the country he came walking back from the village carrying a basket of groceries and a twenty-four-yard coil of rope. She came out to meet him, wiping her hands on her green smock. Her hair was tumbled, her nose was scarlet with sunburn, he told her that already she looked like a barn country woman. His gray flannel shirt stuck to him, his heavy shoes were dusty. She assured him he looked like a rural character in a play. . .

The rural setting makes the characters think, talk, dress as if they fit into the country life. They want to do so, and they redirect their energies toward that end. It is truly a setting that influences behavior, and the author doesn't try to turn up the level of vividness. In fact, there is little description of the rural landscape, even of the home they live in. We know it's the country because the writer says it is, and our imaginations can fill in the blanks that make everything consistent.

The point is that setting can be molded to perform a character-influencing function just as a particular event can. Going back to one of our earlier examples, if we want to portray the barrenness of a character's emotional make-up, we could have the character react to an emotion-urging overture, or. . . we could show the character living in a barren home. Either way the character tells us something about himself/herself:

"Am I supposed to cry because some inattentive mother can't keep her child on the sidewalk? Accidents will always happen. . ."

. . . he was sure there was no dust over the windowsills, just as he was sure the stark, white walls received a daily scrubbing. A home with nothing on the walls but cleanliness, no color, no . . . character, that was it. Even the tiny rug in the middle of the floor was inoffensive in its beigeness. Hardly distinguishable from the floor around it. . .

We may not find the characters likeable, but we do know how they might become so.

Setting can influence character, it really can.

7

Setting As a Plot Limitation

One day a writer begins a story. . .

It was early daylight by the river, and the heavy storms that had passed during the night left a rotting odor. As if the river bottom had turned itself inside out. Campers, cautious with the vagueness of half-sleep, poked through tent slits and wondered at the muddy imprints of the sturdy rains.

A clash of metal on metal parted the stillness. "Hooey! Hooey!" came the nasal voice. "Up we go. . . up and away. . ."

Careful, the writer reminds himself. Don't let the characters take over so soon. Remember where we are.

Woods, thickened from the lush spring, marched close to the river—darkened pines and poplars, leafy ferns and firs embraced one another with healthy ardor. A silver mist hung back from the river's edge, a twinkle against the darkened, loamy monolith.

"Look! Fog," came a whisper from behind a tent slit.

"This ain't the ocean."

"Where are we anyway?"

Metal on metal again. "Ten minutes, boys, all you get today! Up and away, up and away. . ."

The writer pauses. The setting is clear in his mind, but will it be clear to the reader? Deep, thick woods, a group of young boys on a lengthy hike, things happen, no one is unaffected. How massive should the woods be, he wonders? Fifty miles across? That had been his first thought. Make it so huge it would be beyond normal human control. The plot could take so many twists and turns, there would be such wide territory to cover.

What a minute. If no one in the story can control the setting, maybe I can't either. . .

"How far're we hiking today?" A smug question-asker. He already knows the answer, little grin, half-shut eyes. The others put him up to it.

"Maybe the other side of the forest."

"Forget it. No way."

The size of the woods overwhelms the writer. Can his hikers march through this much without the story falling apart? The woods—at least these huge woods—hold too many mysteries and uncertainties for this writer. He feels lost in the massiveness of his undertaking. What to do?

"Hooey!" the raucous shout to attention. "Hooey!"

"Sounds like a bull frog," the smug one whispers to no one special.

"In twos. . . find your partner. . . we're—ah—going up river. . . five, six miles there's a camp I know. Rest there tonight.

"How far's that from the lodge?"

"We can hike out tomorrow. . ."

The writer takes a deep breath. Under control once again, there won't be any trek into wild and woolly wilderness.

Twin questions—what's happening? where am I?—come together when we consider that our setting can have a definite effect on our plot. When our writer decides to redirect the hike, he is placing certain limitations on the plot. The story might have proceeded through arduous adventures, day after day, as the hikers slog through the heavy woods. But by having the hike terminate the next day, the writer narrows the setting from the vast woods to just the portion of it that follows the river to a place of sanctuary for the hikers.

As we truncate the setting, we necessarily limit the plot. It works with every type of story, every type.

Suppose we want to write a mystery. Here's Roy Sorels and Megan Daniel on the interrelationship between setting and plot: "If only a dozen or so characters can qualify as suspects, setting can help provide a reason why the number is limited. In *Ten Little Indians* it's an island; in *Murder on the Orient Express*, a train; in *The Mousetrap*, a snow bound house." Note that the setting is limited physically, and this controls what will happen and to whom it will happen.

For example, if our story is confined to an island, we can have events range across the physical landscape, knowing that the characters can wander—or flee—only so far in any direction. And the characters themselves are limited in number and type because they are the only ones on the island. Look back at our struggling writer: If his story is played out against the huge, uncharted woods, there will be few limitations on his plot, and he must be ever conscious of a tendency for the story to grow unwieldy. But once he tightens up the setting—the hikers now follow the river for a day and a half—he can maintain a tighter hold on what will happen.

Writers have used endlessly the technique of narrowing the setting to control the plot. In the mid-nineteenth century, for example, Emily Brontë developed it for her classic, *Wuthering Heights,* the story of passion and evil and dark suspense on the Yorkshire moors. From the first sentence we understand where the story will be set

My name is Lockwood, and I am a tenant of Thrushcross Grange, belonging to a Mr. Heathcliff, who lives at Wuthering Heights, so called from the bleak and windy character of its site—"wuthering" being a provincial word indicating the tumult of a storm. It is an old farmhouse with the inscription "Hareton Earnshaw, 1580" amid grotesque carvings, over the principal door. . .

From that point the story is controlled by the people in the farmhouse and by the physical dimensions of the farmhouse itself. Whatever happens develops from the setting, and the author is in confident control of her world at all times.

We see the same technique in today's literature. In *Bunco*, a story by Marilyn Jean Conner, the entire action is played out in a nursing home. Once again, from the opening sentence we understand the setting and the limits of the plot:

Mrs. Endsley was paid to keep everyone happy. Her latest project involved composing a Conwoody Convalescent song, something on the order of a school song, but with some of the parts left out. And it was just in her line of duty that, on a Wednesday in early May, just before supper, she sneaked her little silver wand around inside the triangle hanging at one end of the dining room. Thurlow looked on the floor to see if he'd dropped his fork; Delman patted his pockets for his hearing aid; Julia admired a basket of biscuits. But the other forty-four Conwoody Convalescents looked toward Mrs. Endsley and the new girl who stood beside her propped in an aluminum walker. This new girl made forty-eight, optimum occupancy by Mrs. Endsley's reckoning. . .

The plot is already established, the setting nicely carved out; it will be a story of quiet conflict, inmate versus inmate, nursing home staff versus nursing home patients. Whatever happens will occur right there, in Conwoody Convalescent Home, and even by the end of the first paragraph we have a good line on who some of the protagonists will be.

Note that the setting is eminently controllable, in that the entire story is played out against the physical dimensions of the home, its rooms, corridors, dining spaces, public areas and offices. We can manipulate scenes easily in order to accommodate the plot (for example, if one patient wants to slip a note to another, we can have it happen in one of the rooms, in the dining hall or even in the corridor).

The point is this: plot will be influenced by the setting we choose, and if our setting is sharply defined, the plot will necessarily be limited by it.

Physical dimensions, however, are not the only device by which a setting can be established. An island, a ship, a house, even a subway train (see John Godey's *The Taking of Pelham*

One, Two Three, for example) are subjects that seem most appropriate. . . but what about the intangible, something we can't touch or see or smell?

The mind, for instance.

Can a story be set in someone's mind?

Try Edgar Allan Poe's *The Tell-Tale Heart.* It's the story of a murder, but the entire story unweaves from the fixations and obsessions of the narrator, and the reader follows the tortuous path of the narrator's logic as his mind justifies what he has done and why. The narrator's mind is the setting for the story because whatever happens springs from his creations. The narrator has dismembered his victim and placed him beneath the floorboards of the house, but then, three policemen arrive because someone has heard a scream. The narrator begins to have a ringing in his ears, even as the policemen finish a thorough search of the house, and find nothing:

"Yet as the sound increased—and what could I do? I was *a low, dull quick sound—much such a sound as a watch makes when enveloped in cotten.* I gasped for breath—and yet the officers heard it not. I talked more quickly—more vehemently; but the noise steadily increased. I rose and argues about trifles, in a high key, and with violent gesticulations; but the noise steadily increased. Why *would* they not be gone? I paced the floor to and fro with heavy strides, as if excited to fury by the observations of the men—but the noise steadily increased. Oh God! what *could* I do? I foamed—I raved—I swore..."

The entire story plays out in the narrator's mind, from the moment he conceives of the murder to his ultimate confession. The dimensions of his mind are the boundaries of the setting because it is in his mind that the author wants the reader to be. Remember "Where Am I?" If we ask that question here, the answer should be. . . the narrator's mind. It is the foundation for the story, simple as that. The murder itself, the dismemberment of the body and its stashing, the arrival of and search by the policemen are portrayed against the obsessions of the narrator. It is the obsessions which give dimension to the actions, and the obsessions, of course, are the product of the mind.

The plot is limited here, just as if the setting had physical boundaries. What the narrator does or can do or even what the other characters are capable of are controlled by the way the narrator's mind sees things, and while such a setting might seem physically ungraspable, we do understand its limits.

Don't we?

8

Setting As Established by Dialogue

Most of us fall into the trap of assuming that scene setting should begin with a narrative step. . . *The ground was hard, and in the late autumn day, unkempt piles of leaves and twigs rustled in the biting wind. A hunchback-shaped hill loomed over the quiet turf, and a lone figure stared at a wedge-shaped rock that seemed to shoot from the hillside. . .*
Easily done, with physical description and a certain continuity that takes in the various pieces of the scene. There's the ground. . . the time of day. . . the time of year. . . the physical dimensions (a hill, a rock, a human being). . . the stage business (leaves and twigs rustling). . . the climate (a biting wind). All of these, formed together, make up the setting, the answer to *where am I*?
We know where we are, don't we?
But suppose we try to do the same thing, using dialogue in-

stead of narrative? Can the setting be portrayed?

Let's see.

"North wind, tonight," Eph said, hunching himself tighter inside his thick jacket.

"Gettin' hard to see," the old man grumbled. "Road gets bad behind the big hill, there."

"Ground sure froze up fast last week. Early winter, most likely." Eph kicked away some twigs that had blown against his legs, then he looked into the fast-disappearing daylight. "Some day that rock's gonna come unstuck from the hillside."

"Been there a long time," the old man muttered. "My granddaddy said it came all of a sudden one day, right after a big rainstorm washed away part of the hillside. Popped out, kind of."

"Look there! In the field. . ."

"What?. . . oh yeah, what's he doing'?"

"It's a guy, right? Standing there?"

"The rock. Brings all kinds. . ."

The dialogue shows us the same things the narrative tells us; it's a bit longer perhaps, and we have to develop more interrelationship with the characters, but the purpose can be the same: scene setting. Dialogue and narrative can be used with equal effect.

But is there a time when one might be used in place of the other? "There is drama in dialogue, in emotion," said one writer a few years ago, and it's true. Dialogue, by its nature, brings us closer to the characters because we see, hear and feel them speak, we identify or sympathize or reject their words as if they are our own. Where there is tension between characters, and it is portrayed in dialogue, we find ourselves in the middle of the fray too, we are a participant, rather than a spectator.

This is less easily accomplished with narrative because it is being told to us. If the writer tells us the ground is hard (as in the example above), we have a more difficult time imagining ourselves in the middle of the scene. But if we have a character saying "Ground sure froze up quickly last week," we can imagine ourselves part of the conversation. We can sense the hard ground, we could be walking upon it, and we're talking about it.

So, when we want to inject drama into our setting, we might consider using dialogue to set it off. This doesn't mean that narrative can't be equally dramatic, only that dialogue can accomplish it quicker and sometimes with more impact.

The physical dimensions of a setting are what we usually think of when we construct a scene: the landscape, the weather, the nearby objects, their colors, shapes and sizes. It's a framework within which we can paint the storyline. But suppose we want to develop something more intangible, less physical. Suppose we want to create a setting of ideas or values, depending not upon the physical dimensions of the scene but on the substance of a belief—the question of right or wrong, for instance.

Could we do it? Can a setting be based upon such an intangible?

Consider Ernest Hemingway's short story, *Che Ti Dice La Patria?* which deals with two travelers in Fascist Italy in the 1920s. They are stopped by a police officer who tells them the license plate on their car is dirty, even though they know it was just wiped clean.

"I cannot read it. It is dirty."

I wiped it off with a rag.

"How's that?"

"Twenty-five lire."

"What?" I said. "You could have read it. It's only dirty from the state of the roads."

"You don't like Italian roads?"

"They are dirty."

"Fifty lire." He spat in the road. "Your car is dirty, and you are dirty too."

"Good. And give me a receipt with your name."

He took out a receipt book, made it in duplicate, and perforated, so one side could be given to the customer, and the other side filled in and kept as a stub. There was no carbon to record what the customer's ticket said.

"Give me fifty lire."

He wrote in indelible pencil, tore out the slip and handed it to me. I read it.

"This is for twenty-five lire."

"A mistake," he said, and changed the twenty-five to fifty.. . .

Do we need a lot of physical description to understand where we are here? The corruption and the cynicism of the police officer as depicted by his manner with the narrator give us a clear image of the state of morality in Fascist Italy. What's right is what *I* think it is, never mind truth or fairness or simple logic. The dialogue shows a corrupt police officer bullying a traveler for the purpose of extracting some money. Narrative, no matter how skillful, could never depict this scene in precisely this way; it could never give life and drama to the moral give-and-take which sets the scene. We need little of the surrounding physical dimensions in order to be a part of this scene; it is enough that we understand and consume the varying degrees of right and wrong.

Because that is the real setting here—the cynicism and corruption in a totalitarian regime. The entire story plays itself out against that background.

Dialogue value, however, doesn't stop with developing a moral atmosphere. It can reach down to a more specific level and utilize less lofty techniques to accomplish the same purpose. Dialogue can, for example, mingle slang or words of art to create a setting. Buzzwords from any field (technology comes immediately to mind) offer some legitimacy to what is being said:

"We want to fix the cursor before the opfid comes on line."

"What about the technex supply? Bobby'll want mucho gridstain before ETR locks in. . ."

We do enough of this, and a setting is created. We don't need to describe the technology or much of the physical surroundings; the buzzwords make it seem real enough.

See how Robley Wilson, Jr. does it with his story, *Fathers,* about an older man and a younger woman playing golf:

"Why don't we forget about the ball," the young woman said. "Why don't you just take a drop?"

The man, considerably older, was in the short rough just off the seventh fairway. He was walking carefully, looking down, swinging the head of a two-iron across the tops of wild flowers.

"It's a Titleist," he said.

"It's not as if you couldn't afford a new one."

"You just want to add to my score."

"You won't break forty anyway," she said. "Take a drop."

"I can maybe break eighty if we play a second nine." He rested the club on his shoulder and looked broodingly into the scrub pine that separated the seventh fairway from the sixth. "You suppose it's in there?"

"I haven't a clue. You hooked it so badly I couldn't follow it."

"I sliced it," he said. . .

Look at the golf buzzwords in this short passage: "drop". . . "Titleist". . . "break forty". . . "break eighty". . . "second nine". . . "hooked". . . "sliced". . . These particular terms, used by the characters, are much more effective in creating the setting than would be a narrative passage that described the search for the lost ball. The dialogue not only sets up the nature of the scene (golfers playing golf), but also provides insight into the relationship between the golfers (a dogged older man, a bored, impatient younger woman). We see tension between them, and this provides substance to the setting because it allows the characters to dwell on their golf conversation. . . and this creates a more than adequate picture frame for the story.

It's a technique that's readily usable. All we need is a working knowledge of the slang or jargon in a particular slice of life. We pepper that through the dialogue, and we develop a scene dependent upon such portrayal.

Buzzwords do the trick! They really do.

Sometimes, though, we don't need to go that far. Simple tension is all we must have, tension between the characters in some form so that the inherent drama in the scene will burst forth.

Can tension be a setting? No, but it is a technique that will develop the setting. If we want our setting to be more than simple backdrop for the storyline, we have to inject it with some drama, and tension, as any writer knows, is the key to drama.

Tension comes in many forms—human versus human, human versus animal, human versus the spirit—and this is not the place to explore it all. But we must be aware that for dialogue to work, it has to carry tension, and so a setting composed mainly of dialogue must be tension filled, as well.

How better than to place characters in competition with one another? We don't need to elaborate on the physical dimensions because the competitive give-and-take will put the setting together. It is in the dialogue that the setting evolves.

See how Stephan Wolf does it with his *The Legacy of Beau Kremel,* a story about the return of a young adult son to his parents' home in Chicago. He has been away a long time, and within minutes we see his parents vie for his attention and approval. The issue is where they should go to dinner that night, and his mother has offered a suggestion:

"But it's so far," my father complained. "That's halfway to the Loop. What about The Cork over there on Skokie Avenue," and his weighty arm gestured toward the closet.

"Fine."

"I hear the food is terrible," my mother declared.

"No!"

"*Terrible.* Eileen ate there three days ago and nearly got food poisoning," but then she turned to me again and said eagerly,

"Unless you'd like to eat there, dear."

"Doesn't matter. Anyplace is fine."

"How about Fanny's?" my father asked her.

"Fine."

"Should I call for a reservation?" inquired my father."

"Oh, we don't need one," she scoffed. "Unless we go late."

"Are you hungry?" he asked me.

"Starved."

"Why didn't you fix him something?" he asked my mother.

"Do you want me to fix you something?" she asked.

"I can wait," I said to her. . .

Is there an overpowering need to describe the furniture in the room where this action takes place? Do we need to know the time of year, the state of the weather? Do we even need to know if the two parents are sitting or standing when this conversation takes place? Isn't it enough to sense their competitive battling and to see it as the framework for the storyline?

The setting for this scene is the tension between mother and father. What the characters ultimately do—whether they go out for dinner and where they finally go—is the product of that tension or competition. The dialogue sets up the tension and gives it a forum to work itself out, and once again we don't have to be overly concerned with the physical dimensions of the scene.

Where am I?

In the middle of a mother-father spat for the big prize.

A son's approval.

9

Mixing and Matching

Des Moines, Washington. . .
St. Louis, Utah. . .
Baltimore, South Carolina. . .
The familiar and the unfamiliar, cities we know, states we know, but when we combine them, they don't match. Des Moines isn't in Washington, St. Louis isn't in Utah, Baltimore isn't in South Carolina. . .

But they could be! Write a story and set it anywhere; there's no rule that says we have to follow the geographic plot of our trusty atlas. That is, we can mix up one city with another state, set our story and feel free to develop characterizations and events without the limitations a true-to-the-picture setting would require. It affords us breathing space.

"Why would anyone want to do this?" one of my writing

students asks.

"Makes it more creative," another answers.

"Look at William Kennedy's novels," I say, "each one set in Albany, New York. He's writing about a real place."

"Real people, real events," a third student offers.

"Why didn't he mix it up?" I ask. "Set everything in a fictitious place like Albany, Ohio, for example. . ."

"He knows Albany, New York so well."

"He could make it sound authentic."

"He wasn't writing about people who are still alive. . ."

This last pulls a smile from me. "Is that important?"

My original questioner nods with quick certainty. "There's no one who'd complain if he didn't get it right."

"Anonymity," I say, "Kennedy isn't concerned about it. In fact, the more accurate he is, the more authentic his setting, the more we come to know, understand and empathize with the people in the real Albany."

"He didn't mix his settings, then?"

"He didn't need to. . ."

But some writers do need to develop an anonymous setting, somewhere that fingers can't point and accusatory voices can't declare to be true to life. One good reason is to avoid legal troubles, even if there's no intention to paint a person or a reputation with venomous colors. The point is that when we use an existing setting, we are limited by what that setting offers us in terms of place, location, name and surroundings, and we run the risk that—fully without intention—we might stomp on extra-sensitive toes in the course of developing our setting.

    . . . it was a hotel made for the ambitious concierge,
    astride, as it was, the east-west face-offs in Istanbul's
    old city. A concierge who knew his trade (and they

almost always did) could extract hard currency for even the simplest information, and, of course, if some surreptitious photography were needed, he could remain behind his behemoth of a counter, survey and photograph comings and goings through the small lens that poked through his official concierge pin. . .

Suppose we set this story in a real Istanbul hotel, and we name the hotel, though we avoid naming the concierge. . . do we have problems?

We could. If there is a concierge at the real hotel, he could certainly complain about the portrayal, even though we don't identify him by name. Other people would know, however, simply because we kept the details authentic.

So what do we do? Use the hotel name, if we wish, but set the story in Oslo, Norway or Athens, Greece. Pick a spot, anywhere but Istanbul.

Then mix and match. Des Moines, Washington. . . St. Louis, Utah... . Baltimore, South Carolina. . .

Anonymity is what we're after.

But it's not the only reason to mix and match. In fact, mixing and matching is more than plucking one city or town or location and weaving it into another location, more than simply trying to hide authenticity. Mixing and matching is also a useful stylistic tool when we develop our setting. It can be a way to build drama and reader interest.

Here is the opening to Sinclair Lewis's fine novel, *Babbitt,* set in the town of Zenith in the upper midwestern United States during the 1920s. Lewis sets the broad scene in just two paragraphs:

> The towers of Zenith aspired above the morning mist; austere towers of steel and cement and limestone, sturdy as cliffs and delicate as silver rods.

They were neither citadels nor churches, but frankly and beautifully fine buildings.

The mist took pity on the fretted structures of earlier generations: the Post Office with its shingle-tortured mansard, the red brick minarets of hulking old houses, factories with stingy and sooted windows, wooden tenements colored like mud. The city was full of such grotesqueries, but the clean towers were thrusting them from the business center, and on the farther hills were the shining new houses, homes—they seemed—for laughter and tranquility...

What we have here is mixing and matching in the stylistic sense—using different, contrasting settings to develop the complete picture. Note the first paragraph: "The towers. . . aspired. . .," ". . . delicate as silver rods. . .," ". . . beautifully fine buildings." All of this paints a portrait of serenity, of pleasure for the eye to behold.

But then in the second paragraph: "The mist took pity. . .," ". . . shingle-tortured mansard. . .," ". . . hulking old houses. . .," ". . . stingy and sooted windows. . .," ". . . tenements colored like mud." No serenity here, no pleasure for the eye to behold. The opposite, in fact. Ugliness and depression, what Lewis calls "grotesqueries." The flip side of the paragraph that precedes it.

These contrasts clearly give an immediate conflict in the narrative, and in so doing, help build the drama. Conflict, tension, these are basic writer's tools, and when we can develop such techniques while simultaneously accomplishing another purpose (such as building our setting) we can consider ourselves fortunate. The truth is, however, that mixing and matching settings in the way Sinclair Lewis does it is not overly difficult. For example:

— if the setting is a forest, contrast the eeriness of the
   darkened tree shapes to the innocence of young
   children following a narrow, uncertain path.
— if the setting is a cruise ship, contrast the well-
   appointed upper-deck spaces with the over-used,
   aged engine spaces below deck.
— if the setting is a ski area, contrast the beautifully
   manicured ski trails with the diabolical plans of a
   real-estate developer who wants to turn it all into
   condos. . .

Contrasts in settings.

It doesn't even need to be on a broad landscape, either.
Contrast will work within the framework of any scene — a
passenger compartment in a train, a back table in a coffee
shop, the floor of the New York Stock Exchange.

Anywhere. See how it works within the walls of a fine old
home. These two paragraphs are from *Trinity*, Leon Uris's
novel about 3 generations of Irish and English in Northern
Ireland during the late nineteenth and early twentieth century. He is describing the interior of Rathweed Hall, the
magnificent manor house:

[The first mistress] established the house's pre-
eminence in white Paonazzetto marble, delicately
veined and hued with pink and purple strands, a daz-
zle that shouted its name and uniqueness to all of
Ulster. The main floor, halls, stairs, salons and col-
umns ran heavily to Paonazzetto, then deepened
dramatically into darker breccias and verde anticos in
the master suite on the upper floors. What might have
been a preponderance of marble was broken by twenty thousand square feet of Sasonnerie carpets, each
designed to offset its particular area. . .

91

And less than one page later, still on the interior:
Forays to Venice and Spain burst Hieronymus Bosch
and Goya into his life. In bizarre contrast to the clean
villa lines of the house and its understatement came a
legion of tortured naked bodies, satanists, monsters
in the throes of perversions, black masses, grotesque
satires of semi-men/semi-beasts.. . .
Such beauty and such grossness all within the same home,
all within the same setting. Lovely, quiet colors in conflict
with harsh, unsettling figures; subdued marble and woodwork at war with wall hangings that shouted obscenities.

Is this drama? Is this more interesting than reading through
a one-dimensional home-furnishings description where
everything conforms and nothing breaks ranks? Don't we
feel an edge of excitement?

The setting contrasts tell us something will happen in that
house. It has to. It sets the scene—it *makes* the scene, and the
way events occur and characters behave will follow naturally.

The equation is simple. . . contrast = conflict = drama.

And every story *must* have drama.

We mix and match to accomplish this, but that's not all we
seek to create. Through our use of setting-drama we can build
depth and substance in our story, in the characters, and in the
overall scene. Using setting-contrasts doesn't mean we stop
once we develop drama; now we have to mold it and shape it,
we have to provide it with substance.

It isn't enough to describe a breathtaking building towering
over a filthy, rat-infested garbage dump; we have to show
why it is there, what purpose it serves in the story, how it will
affect events. Developing the setting-contrast means little
unless we plan to use it to bolster the story. Otherwise it's like
a leftover stage prop the curtain forgot to hide.

In William Goldman's novel, *Brothers*, note how the setting-contrast provides us with a sense of the importance to the story of the Café du Monde. Note, too, how Goldman depicts his setting-contrast in stylistic form, using negatives to imply positives rather than adopting straight narrative.

His protagonist, Scylla, contemplates the Café du Monde:

The Café du Monde was not a gastronomic palace. And he had dined at many of the world's great bistros. Harry's in Venice, Durgin-Park in Beantown, El Parador's in Manhattan. He adored bistros, Scylla did.

The Café du Monde could not even qualify as that.

And since, when you Provided for Division, living was always first-class, no wine list had ever daunted him. So, yes, he'd had the '61 Palmer, many times, and the '47 Cheval Blanc, in magnum, if you please, and the '31 Norval, beyond argument the greatest wine of the century.

The Café du Monde didn't have a wine list. It didn't really have a menu. What it served was café au lait and beignets. Period. You could have milk if you wanted to. So why had it survived for so long with nothing but chicory coffee and crispy fried rectangular doughnuts, topped with powdered sugar?

Because it had weight. It was a *place*. . .

Don't we get a sense of the importance of the Café du Monde from the fact that Scylla was there for reasons other than the food or the wine list? If he wanted a fine meal, he would be elsewhere—hence there must be something or someone here he seeks. By using negatives to establish what the café is not, we can also sense what it is—a café that exists for reasons other than its food and wine. It is subtle contrast, to be sure, but it does the job of establishing a purpose for the cafe, and it provides depth and substance to the scene. Now we know—at least we think we know—that something important will happen.

Why?

Because Scylla is here, and he's not looking for a good meal.

We mix and match to develop drama out of ordinary description, and as we see, there are several ways it can be done. The important thing to remember is this:

Mix and match with a purpose.

When it works, an entire scene can come alive.

10

Using Time to Establish the Setting

Is there something significant about midnight. . . dawn. . .noon. . .dusk? Does an image appear?

Midnight. . . blackness, eerie sounds, foreboding, shadows, strangers, blowing wind. . .

or

Midnight. . . laughter, music, dancing, full moon, excitement, anticipation. . .

Sometimes we can set our story with the notion that the time of its occurrence should influence where and when the story takes place. For example, our scene is to take place at dawn. Would it be appropriate to have things happen in a corporate boardroom at that time? Or a movie theatre?

Only if the characters are there because they need unrestrained privacy, and they must act without delay.

But we can do better!

Dawn. . . quiet, cool, streaky sky, shiny, new things, clear thoughts. . .

The characters need unrestrained privacy. Put them in an automobile on an uncrowded highway, have them explore their thoughts without speaking. Dawn is a good time for all that. See how Alice Adams handles it with the opening of her story, *Molly's Dog*, and note how the time of day establishes not only where she is (her car) but what's in her mind:

Accustomed to extremes of mood, which she experienced less as "swings" than as plunges, or more rarely as soarings, Molly Harper, a newly retired screenwriter, was nevertheless quite overwhelmed by the blackness—the horror, really, with which, one dark pre-dawn hour, she viewed a minor trip, a jaunt from San Francisco to Carmel, to which she had very much looked forward. It was to be a weekend, simply, at an inn where in fact she had often stayed before, with various lovers (Molly's emotional past had been strenuous). This time she was to travel with Sandy Norris, an old non-lover friend, who owned a bookstore. . . This trip, she realized, too late, at dawn, was to represent a serious error in judgment, one more in a lifetime of dark mistakes. It would weigh down and quite possibly sink her friendship with Sandy. . .

Dawn. . . special truths that seem more easily faced, more honestly explored. At this hour she is able to gauge the staying power of her friendship with Sandy, and she knows it will not last. She sees the trip as "horror," and the pre-dawn blackness gives it substance; then at dawn, when first light comes, she comes to realize that the trip is a mistake. In the blackness of pre-dawn is the emotion ("horror"), and in the light of dawn is the unemotional conclusion.

The time of day establishes what she thinks, how she thinks it and what the outcome will be. The setting—and the time of day—provide the framework for her to do her thinking.

Dawn is a good time for clear thinking, and that's what Alice Adams's character is doing.

Try another. This time we'll use the flashback technique to pinpoint the time of day we want to highlight. . . *She recalled her father's funeral more than twenty years ago, a strange morning with the snow falling and the sun out, a wisp of spring in the air but thick ice on the porch steps. . .*

An early spring morning, and we have a setting that fits the time.

See how Lee K. Abbott does it with his story, *X,* and the recollections of a man about one day in his youth:

> I was seventeen then, a recent graduate of our high school (where I now teach mathematics and coach JV football), and on the afternoon in question I had been sitting at the edge of the Club pool, baking myself in the summer sunshine we are famous for. I was think-ing—as I suspect all youths do—about the wonder I would become. I had a girlfriend, Pammy Jo (my wife now), a '57 Ford Fairlane 500 (yellow over black), and the knowledge that what lay before me seemed less future than fate—which is what happens when you are raised apart from the big world of hor-ror and cross-heartedness; yet, at the moment I'd glimpsed the prize I would be—and the way it is in the storybooks I read—disaster struck...

It is a summer afternoon in his character's youth, and the flashback pinpoints the time period: a lazy hour, the character quite full of himself, calmness before a sudden

97

storm. Disaster often comes when we least expect it and in a form we least expect (in Abbott's story it is the youth's father who suddenly goes berserk on the golf course, assaulting and menacing others and finally destroying the golf club locker room). This moment, when the young man feasts on himself, is the perfect setting for the intrusion of disaster, a change of pace which makes the disaster all the more poignant because it contrasts so vividly with the moment of self-satisfaction the youth revels in.

Would it be the same if the father went berserk at midnight. . .or dawn? Probably not, because a flashback to those moments wouldn't have a man on the golf course or a young man at the edge of a pool. And while we could try to create a setting where the young man revels in his own self-image, midnight or dawn are difficult moments for this purpose when he's sitting by the edge of a swimming pool.

But not a hot summer afternoon. That's *the* time for things like this to happen.

A flashback, a moment, a setting.

Suppose we want to use a transition to establish a *passage* of time instead of a single moment? Suppose we want to jump the action a few moments or hours or days? We need to bring the curtain down on one scene and open it to another:

— "Later we went to. . ."
— "Next day we decided. . ."
— "Twenty minutes into the game the rains came. . ."

The transition serves to move the action along; it also serves to show the movement of time so that we don't get bogged down with nonessentials and irrelevancies. As the transition progresses, we—the readers—get a fix on the new setting, and at the end of the transition, we should be in tune with the writer: "Where are we?" should not be a mystery.

Three hours later the water level had come up to the window ledges on the first floor, and the rains seemed harder than ever. We could imagine everything afloat downstairs, even grandmother's silkscreen cushion that my mother hated so much. . .

The passage of time shows us that the situation of the characters has become more critical, that the setting for the story has become more dangerous. The characters haven't changed locations during the transition, so the setting itself isn't any different.

But it's not the same, either. Now, things are more suspenseful, and the setting becomes a more important character in the story. What the *passage* of time has done is to change the emphasis of the story, and in doing this it has made the setting ever more crucial.

Of course, transitions can also change the setting:

— Three hours later we came to a clearing in the woods. . .

— Later, we took a drive in Uncle Hilly's convertible. . .

— That evening the party had already reached the raucous stage when we arrived. . .

A transition, a *passage* of time, a change of setting.

The movement of time operates in more than just transitions. Suppose we want to develop a setting out of a broad landscape:

Far off, almost scraping the bottom of the clouds were the sharp peaks of the inner range, their huge slopes shadowed and indistinct. Lines of vegetation crisscrossed the lower levels, and tiny road-trails snaked through the heavy growth. The inner range

ran across the horizon, blocking forward progress
across a one hundred twenty-degree expanse. . .

Here, time moves slowly because we are introducing a big, wide setting, and the elements have to come along one by one. As we discover each element of this broad landscape time seems almost to stand still, and the story itself seems on hold—at least until we get through the setting description.

But we can accelerate time within our story by increasing the tempo of our setting description:

A darkened room, a glint in the corner, shadows,
neon flashes, the scrape of a chair, a stifled breath,
quiet movement to the door, knife ready, eyes sharp,
a bed somewhere on the left, thick chair to the
side. . .

Doesn't time seem to leap forward with this setting? The discovery of each element of the setting at a quickened pace serves to speed the time along, and this, in turn, establishes our setting. That room—and the setting—are full of suspense. We build the suspense by having the characters discover each element in the setting and at a pace which excites and dramatizes. If we didn't want to build suspense in the scene, we might have the setting somewhere else, and we might have the characters discover things in a more leisurely fashion, such as in the example of the broad landscape.

But where we want time to speed up, we do so by having our setting introduced in a more rapid manner. The key is tempo—how fast do we want things to happen?

Slow—a leisurely description of the setting.

Fast—a quick, sometimes jumbled, disorderly description of the setting.

Part B

Mood and Atmosphere

Prelude

A sense of place. We discussed it in connection with setting, and we know it as our experiences and memories coming
together to form a foundation for who we are and where we
come from. In terms of setting it tends to be limited to a
geographic area—our hometown, for instance, or a certain
house or street and we are able to describe it in fairly simple,
straightforward terms:

The island was shaped like a partially devoured ice
cream cone, with both ends eaten away not hiding the
original shape. .

But a sense of place—to be fully developed—actually has
a second side. Giving it a geographical location is like putting
together the framework, the outline; what we have to do next
is to fill in the flesh and blood. We have to breathe some life
into it.

How?

We develop mood and atmosphere so that the sense of place pulses and throbs! It's no longer over *there*, now it's here, around us, through us, under us, over us. It exists because we feel it and breathe it.

The techniques for developing mood and atmosphere are based on the creation of emotion, not only within the characters on the written page but within the reader as well. These emotions, if sculpted properly, should provide depth and substance when we answer the question "where are we?"

Take a restaurant scene where two lovers are conversing. Suppose we want to show a sensuous side to their relationship. We could do that with dialogue, but perhaps they aren't the type of people who find it comfortable to express their feelings that way. Why, then, couldn't we set the scene by adding sensory details to the basic physical setting? For example:

. . . creamy, damask table cloth, velvety smooth, unwrinkled; delicate orchid scents misting from soft-lit walls, hushed voices and purple-red carpeting, glassware tinkling in graceful witness. . .

Now it's not just a restaurant, it's an experience, and the mood we've created gives flesh and blood to the scene. Obviously, not all mood and atmosphere would be as vivid as this, but the point is that once we add emotional content to the bare bones of our setting we are able to make the scene do many more things.

We can buttress the emotional state of the characters, as we did above; we can add conflict; we can introduce a change of pace so the storyline will perk up; we can develop different points of view from the same set of facts; we can beautify (denigrate too!) a bare-bones geographic scene. . . and more.

By injecting mood and atmosphere into our scene we provide dimension to our story, and the reader can't help but feel a greater kinship to our words and phrases. It's as if we've taken the reader into our confidence, saying "Now this is what we *really* mean, this is what we want you to feel. Isn't it more exciting?"

Perhaps the easiest way to imagine mood and atmosphere is in connection with a sense of place. Think of the metaphors and similes we use to describe our emotional state:
— in a black hole of depression
— high as a kite
— cozy as a bug in a rug
— on the road to self-destruction

Place-names give us a foundation which we can then use to describe the human mind, body and behavior. If we write "as tough as the sidewalks of New York," we know something about the mood of our character or the atmosphere of the locale for the action. If we write "he's in a rut," we know the emotional deprivation our character is going through, and we can then use other techniques, such as dialogue, to expand upon this emotional state.

Look at it this way: if we break down the phrase "sense of place," the "place" part would be aligned with *setting* and the "sense" part with *mood and atmosphere,* so that a complete answer to "where are we?" must explore these two aspects of the phrase. That doesn't mean we *must* explore both, because in any given situation, a setting without mood and atmosphere might serve our purposes. But we should be aware that mood and atmosphere go hand-in-hand with setting when we wish to add emotional importance to our physical framework.

The techniques for using mood and atmosphere are varied,

some appropriate for one situation, some for another. Each, however, if properly used (and by that I mean if its purposes are properly *understood*), will enhance our story and give the reader added pleasure. We'll see how mood and atmosphere influence our story writing so that we learn to develop more skillful story telling, so that we write with consistency and rhythm, so that we expand our use of the techniques into areas such as the creation of nostalgia and the writing of generic fiction.

Think of mood and atmosphere as the artist might think of his pallet; the colors are at his fingertips, the canvas is framed, the lines are sketched, and what he must do is choose which colors will fit between which lines.

In the end it is emotion we seek to produce.

A mood within an atmosphere.

11

Sensory Details, Sensory Images

Is this passage well written?

> The woman walked out of the house and stared at the
> sky. She was distraught because her husband had told
> her he wanted to leave after twenty-four years of mar-
> riage. . .

There's obvious conflict and the beginning of a plot line,
the characters are defined quickly, and we have a general idea
of setting. All good and proper technique.

But. . . somehow the passage doesn't work.

Try this:

> The woman stumbled out of the house and stared at
> the thickening sky, thinking she would be better off
> dead. Her husband's words throbbed inside her head,
> she could taste sour bile. . . *I want out of the mar-
> riage!* he had said. *Now! Today!*

The smell of fear confronted her, she could feel her
skin burn. . .

See the difference? In the first passage we are *telling* our
story, and there is little to spark the reader's imagination. If
we carried this along for several more paragraphs, the reader
would probably lose interest because we haven't given emotions a chance to get activated. We haven't allowed the reader
to get inside the story, to live and breathe, feel and smell with
the characters.

In short, we haven't allowed the reader to become part of
the story.

The second passage, however, does try to do this. Note the
use of image-provoking words and phrases: . . . "stumbled"
. . . "thickening" . . . "words throbbed" . . . "taste sour
bile" . . . "smell of fear" . . . "feel her skin burn" . . .

These words and phrases are an appeal to our sensory
selves, they attempt to make us *feel* what the characters feel
and to become a full partner in the mood and atmosphere
that the writer has designed.

In short, again, sensory perceptions are what make up
mood and atmosphere:

— if we want to show a character in fear, we have
  him/her taste sour bile
— if we want to show at atmosphere of defiance, we
  have characters staring one another down

Using sensory techniques is not difficult, but we have to
train ourselves to apply them properly. First of all we have to
think in sensory details. . . what are those items in our setting
which will appeal to the senses?

A stone wall, perhaps?

Or a pock-marked ridge of gray-black rock with velvety
moss?

The last selection works better, doesn't it? It appeals to our imaginations, we can feel the wall's texture, sense its age and sturdiness. From this we develop atmosphere. . . an air of strength and lonely beauty which will influence the characters and the storyline.

Once we decide upon the sensory details we wish to highlight, then we concentrate on the sensory images we want to invoke. If we wish our readers to feel delight, we use sensory details that will accomplish that (such as a dripping ice cream cone or sparkling sunset or soaring violin solo); if we wish our readers to feel unsettled, we invoke other images (such as a fog-shrouded road or eerie melody or musky, wild-animal scent). Note that these images all appeal to our senses. . . taste, smell, touch, hearing, seeing. These are where the sensory images are received, and these are what the writer strives to touch.

"Nudging the reader's senses" is the way one novelist portrays it; "the senses must be invoked" is the way another says it; "the writer must deal in sense detail" is what a third believes. Other writers might use slightly different words or phrases, but they would agree that for the reader to have a meaningful reading experience, the writer must make that reader feel what the characters feel and slide right into the middle of the story.

Otherwise, the reader will blink and say, so what? Big deal! Boring. . . and the book will slam shut.

See how Thomas Mann handles sensory details in this passage from his *Confessions of Felix Krull, Confidence Man.* Mann is describing one single room, but note how he appeals to our senses:

> It was a narrow room, with a rather high ceiling, and crowded from floor to ceiling with goodies. There

were rows and rows of hams and sausages of all
shapes and colors—white, yellow, red and black; fat
and lean and round and long—rows of canned
preserves, cocoa and tea, bright translucent glass bot-
tles of honey, marmalade and jam. . . I stood enchanted, straining my ears and breathing in the
delightful atmosphere and the mixed fragrance of
chocolate and smoked fish and earthy truffles. . .
And my mouth literally began to water like a
spring. . .

There are many, many sensory details here, all relating to
the foodstuffs on the shelves, and we get a clear picture of the
narrator's delight at what he perceives. The atmosphere, at
this moment in the story, is one of sensuous pleasure, and the
reader shares that because the senses are "nudged". . . the
narrator (and the reader) sees. . . smells. . . hears. . .
tastes. . . and what emerges is a pleasurable experience made
all the more so because we find ourselves standing in the narrator's shoes. If he stands enchanted, so do we. . . if he
strains his ears, so do we. . . if he breathes in the delightful
atmosphere, so do we. . . if his mouth begins to water, so
does ours. . .

Where are we?

In effect, we are in the middle of the story. In a room
packed with delectable food, enjoying ourselves immensely.

But. . . what if the scene takes place in the past, suppose
we have to reconstruct something from history? Does it help
to make an appeal to the senses?

Here's novelist Mary Stewart: ". . . the dynamic use of setting is a weapon that no historical novelist can afford to ignore. To describe scenes, dresses, ways of life of a different
age, may make the story move like a pageant in front of us;

but to take us alive into another period of time, the senses must be invoked.''

The senses must be invoked!

Even when we're writing about times we have no personal experience with, the senses must be invoked. We appeal to sight, sound, touch, taste and smell. History, the future, other worlds, other mindsets, it doesn't matter. The senses make it all come alive.

See how E.L. Doctorow makes a sensory appeal in his novel *Ragtime*, a story set in the first few years of this century. He has Sigmund Freud arriving in New York in 1902 and met by some of his supporters. They show him Central Park, the Metropolitan Museum, Chinatown, and then. . .

> The party went to one of the silent films so popular in stores and nickelodians around the city. White smoke rose from the barrels of rifles and men wearing lipstick and rouge fell backwards clutching their chests. At least, Freud thought, it is silent. What oppressed him about the New World was its noise. The terrible clatter of horses and wagons, the clanking and screeching of streetcars, the horns of automobiles. . .

Note the sensory details and sensory images at work here. We have glimpses of silent films and traffic on the streets, but if these details are left uncharacterized, the passage will read more like a report than an imaginative scene:

> There were silent films to attend and the streets were filled with horses and wagons, streetcars and automobiles. . .

Instead, Doctorow appeals to our senses, and by doing this the entire scene comes alive. We *see* the silent films and the white smoke and men wearing lipstick and rouge. . . we *hear* the clatter of horses and wagons, the clanking and screeching of the streetcars, the horns of automobiles. Our senses are activated, and now we're in the middle of the scene.

There's something else to note, as well. If our senses are going to be teased, the writer must do more than list the details of the scene. There may be horses and wagons, but what makes them effective as a sensory image-maker is that they clatter! The streetcars are only one dimensional until they clank and screech! The silent films don't live for us unless they show white smoke and men with lipstick and rouge.

In short, the writer must *think* images even as he or she lists details on the page. Is a chair only a chair or should it be "smoothly finished wine mahogony"? Do horses trot by or do they "snort and give off a hayfield odor"? Is a restaurant interior softly lit and pleasant or does it have "a velvety feel, a scent of jasmine and an appearance of muted elegance"?

These are sensory images, and the reader will thank us for letting him or her take them to heart.

What we strive for is to develop mood and atmosphere so that our story can proceed in a meaningful way. When we create sensory images for the reader, we provide a means for mood and atmosphere to emerge. The more our characters sense and feel, the more the reader will sense and feel; and the more that happens, the easier it will be for mood and atmosphere to prevail.

For example, in James Dickey's novel, *Deliverance,* four men decide to take a canoe trip down a wilderness river, stopping each night on the river banks to pitch camp. Each has his own tent, and on the first night, the narrator is awakened by a flapping noise just outside. He realizes it is an owl:

In the middle of this sound the tent shook; the owl

had hold of it in the same place. I knew this before I cut the light on—it was still in my hand, exactly as warm as I was—and saw the feet, with the heel talons now coming in. I pulled one hand out of the sleeping bag and saw it wander frailly up through the thin light until a finger touched the cold reptilian nail of one talon below the leg-scales. I had no idea whether the owl felt me; I thought perhaps it would fly, but it didn't. Instead, it shifted its weight again, and the claws on the foot I was touching loosened again...

It's pitch black, the middle of the night, a wilderness area. . . how does Dickey develop mood and atmosphere? By appealing to our—and the character's—sense of sight (the owl talons through the tent), a sense of touch (the cold, reptilian nail of the talon), sense of hearing (the tent shakes).

What mood and atmosphere do we get? Eerie uncertainty, a whisper of danger, burgeoning fear. Our senses tell us these things, and the writer can then take it from there.

The senses must be invoked.

Otherwise, what we'll get is a black and white still life.

Instead of a feature-length film.

12

Varieties of Generic Fiction

A man and woman are in the darkened living room of a large house set along a wind-whipped rocky coastline. It is close to midnight, and the man and woman must now take some action. We know this much. . .the atmosphere of the scene will be crucial to the continuation of the storyline.

What happens next?

We think over techniques for developing that proper atmosphere, but we know it depends on. . . the type of story we are doing.

If it's literary fiction, we have wide latitude with that atmosphere because the only rules we need follow are to keep the atmosphere relevant and well-portrayed (meaning: well-written). It needn't be especially dramatic and it needn't be especially immediate.

But it does need to make us appreciate how that writer uses

words and what he/she has us think about.

The literary story is a "type" of story only in the sense that it is different from what we call "category" fiction or "generic" fiction. Except for the rules above, the literary-story writer is free to create whatever atmosphere he/she wants using any subject he/she wants and having it perform whatever task he/she wants.

Not so with category fiction. Here, the atmosphere (and the mood) are carefully controlled so as to give maximum effect to the category the story hopes to fill. In other words, if it's a suspense story we're writing, we want to keep a suspenseful atmosphere rolling through the story; otherwise, the drama and the storyline might well fall flat.

How many categories are there? David Madden, a few years ago, listed about 65, though some are rarely used and others don't fit the mold very well. He even goes so far as to say, "Characteristics of the types sometimes overlap; none of the types is pure; each type includes aspects of others. . ."

Yet his point should be understood: there are a lot of categories for fiction writing out there, and by and large each category attempts to treat its material differently, and each category has certain aspects which it shares with no other.

For example, let's look at our man and woman in the darkened living room in the house along the rocky coastline. Remember, now, it is close to midnight. . .

How could the atmosphere be portrayed if the category is:
    a suspense story?
    a romance?
    a horror story?

Each should create something different. The suspense story might have the couple waiting to meet someone who will give them valuable or dangerous information, and so the scene would progress to their anticipation of the meeting as well as to the meeting itself. The romance might have the couple finally alone and suddenly realizing they have a strong attraction for one another, and so the scene might progress to initial denial of that attraction, some angry words, further emotional outpouring and final recognition of that attraction. The horror story might have the couple arriving at the house independent of one another because they had each received an intriguing invitation, and so the scene might progress from their curiosity about one another and the house to a search of the deserted house to the sudden intervention of strange sounds and to ominous discoveries. . .

Suspense, romance, horror. These are the categories and these are the atmospheres the particular stories will portray. The purpose is to intrigue the reader and make him or her experience a variety of emotions, depending upon the category, but at all times to make that reader "feel" the story and "experience" the drama.

Category or generic fiction works only if it succeeds in doing this. Leave the thinking and the contemplating and the philosophizing to the literary mainstream. . . the atmosphere of generic fiction must help the reader live what is happening on the pages.

Let's take a look at a suspense story and see the appeal it has for the reader. In Clive Cussler's book, *Deep Six,* a bank clerk, Estelle Wallace, has stolen more than one hundred thousand dollars and fled on an ocean liner bound for foreign anonymity. What she doesn't know is that the ship, itself, is about to be taken over by a handful of its crew, and one evening, after dinner, as she is reclining in her cabin, a crew member, Lee, walks in, picks her up bodily and carries her on deck. It's obvious she has been mildly drugged from dinner because she offers no resistance as he places her down:

> Lee was leaning over her, doing something to her feet. She could feel nothing, only a lethargic numbness. He appeared to be attaching a length of rusty chain to her ankles.
>
> Why would he do that? She wondered vaguely. She watched indifferently as she was lifted into the air. Then she was released and floated through the darkness.
>
> Something struck her a great blow, knocking the breath from her lungs. A cool, yielding force closed over her. A relentless pressure enveloped her body and dragged her downward, squeezing her internal organs in a giant vise.
>
> Her eardrums exploded. . .

The atmosphere is one of fear, uncertainty, pain, shock and ultimate terror as she succumbs to drowning. We, the readers, see her helplessness and know what is coming, yet until the very moment of death we continue to hope something will intervene and save her. That is suspense. . . the anticipation that she might be saved or the concern that once the crew has taken over the ship what will happen next? Why are they doing it, what do they want to accomplish? We know they will not stop at murder to get what they want, so that, as the story progresses and others show up to face them, we anticipate a fearful struggle. Violence and death are sure to follow.

But note the elements of suspense that help to create the atmosphere: she's helpless and someone is taking advantage of that; she's going to be killed and there is no one around to save her; she's in deep pain and there appears to be no relief. . .

In short, we anticipate what's going to happen to her, and we hope it won't.

There's another category of fiction that has had a long—though uneven—tradition. It possesses an atmosphere that, at times, can be highly charged.

Erotic literature, sexually explicit literature. It is a category that writers as diverse as Mark Twain, Vladimir Nabokov, Erica Jong and Anais Nin have worked in. It shouldn't be confused with pornographic writing which carries absolutely no literary merit and debases both writer and subject. Erotic literature is different: the main story line is more than simply a vehicle for the sexual gymnastics, it offers a conscious plot, characterization and a theme. It is, in truth, *a story*.

But erotic literature remains a member of the category-fiction family because one of its main appeals is to our erotic desires. It wants us to feel what the characters are feeling, and in this instance that is sexual arousal.

So the atmosphere for such stories must be sprinkled with techniques that bring about sexual arousal.

One of the most controversial—and erotic—pieces of literature of this century is *Lady Chatterly's Lover* by D.H. Lawrence. In many ways it is more substantial than category fiction because the story deals with much more than the flowering of erotic desires, and Lawrence's prose is stylistically far above that of most category-fiction works.

That, however, doesn't mean the story isn't erotically charged. For instance, take this description of the moment when Connie Chatterly, the sexually repressed heroine, and Mellors, the gamekeeper, reach the zenith of lovemaking joy:

Then as he began to move, in the sudden helpless orgasm, there awoke in her new strange trills rippling, inside her. Rippling, rippling, rippling, like a flapping overlapping of soft flames, soft as feathers, running to points of brilliance, exquisite, exquisite and meeting her all molten inside. It was like bells rippling up and up to a culmination. She lay unconscious of the wild little cries she uttered at the last. . .

All of this so we can *feel* what the characters are feeling, so we can enjoy or suffer with them. Lawrence makes the atmosphere erotic, and he does it with poetic touches. He has his words simulate a couple in the throes of exciting lovemaking. . .

— interior rhyming ("flapping overlapping")
— alliteration ("soft flames, soft as feathers")
— repetitive words ("rippling, rippling, rippling"; "exquisite, exquisite"; "up and up")

Note the rhythm of his phrasing, the pace quickening as the couple grow more excited. . . all to stimulate the reader to become a part of the scene.

He doesn't use four-letter words, and he doesn't try to describe every physical event. He *hints*, and he *touches*, and he lets our imaginations soar. With this category of fiction we don't need a blueprint. . .

Only a sketch.

The same could be said of another category—that of horror writing. Vampires, monsters, other-worldly demons, inexplicable events controlled from afar, all of which are directed at unsuspecting humans, and all of which are immediate and deadly. Here's how J.N. Williamson, a practitioner of this fiction category, describes the horror-writer's technique:

The finer talents in horror constantly *hint* at their readers, slyly suggest that—any page now—an inexorable build-up will begin to that climactic revelation, terrible deed or unbearable force they've hitherto shown in *flashes*. . .

This is atmosphere creation, the development of unease in the characters *and* in the readers. The unease becomes deeper and deeper until. . . Here's Williamson again:

> [It may be] nothing more ominous than rats, restlessly scuttling, dogs barking, growling, howling; drifting snow, unexpected rainfall, glaring noontime sun, shadows with *no source*. . .

Then the horrible event occurs, and the readers feel the terror because the atmosphere, the mood, has turned that way. The horror-writer's task is to develop the unease first, and if it's done through hints, as Williamson advises, then the explosion of horror will follow nicely. See how Joseph Citro, in his book, *Guardian Angels,* accomplishes the hints and suggestions. Will, a fifteen-year-old boy, and his family have moved into a house where four people were slaughtered some years before. One evening Will decides to investigate the attic of the house:

Something skittered across the roof, rapid little claws that must belong to a squirrel.

Startled, Will stood up. He held his breath, eyes aimed at the ceiling. Straining his ears, he listened for every sound in the shadow-filled attic.

The fan whirred. A grating creak sounded from somewhere in the shadows, no doubt the house groaning under his own weight.

Tense now, the hairs on the back of his neck prickling, Will had the uncomfortable impression that someone was close by, hiding, watching.

He looked around, not daring to venture another step.

Old houses made noises, he reasoned. But an irrational echo came back: *old houses are haunted. . .*

The writer is hinting, hinting, hinting here, isn't he? Several events occur, one after the other, unseen but heard or felt, and the explanation could be, might be. . . that the house is haunted!

What's that mean to us, the readers? Strange events could be unfolding, ghosts and the other-worldly figures might be around, might be a menace to Will and his family. The atmosphere is charged with uncertainty, unease, danger and strangeness. It is the prelude to the explosion of the horrible event that gives this category its name.

Horror-writers hint, horror-writers suggest. . . and the reader worries along with the characters. The atmosphere is fear of the unknown which then controls what the characters say and do.

While horror-writers work to make us uneasy, writers who specialize in romance fiction work equally as hard to make us joyful and sad. Romance fiction is concerned with the emotional relationship between the characters, and it rises and falls on how romantically that relationship can be portrayed. The old saw. . . boy meets girl, boy loses girl, boy finds girl. . . with certain variations and refinements, is the basic plot of this category, but in order to make it all work, the mood and atmosphere of the story must carry the reader right along. Emotions must be strong, strong, strong! People have to *feel*, events have to inspire or devastate.

And if the characters find themselves in a romantic interlude, the romance had better be sensuous and exciting. Take a look at Danielle Steele's *Fine Things,* the story of a divorcée, Liz, and Bernie, a department store manager. After several meetings, they find themselves deeply attracted to one another, and Bernie proposes marriage. It is now the next evening, and they have decided to spend the night together for the first time.

The elevator rose to the top floor, and Liz followed him to a door directly across the hall without saying a word. He took a key from his pocket and let her inside. It was the most beautiful suite she had ever seen, in a movie or in real life, or ever even dreamed of. Everything was white and gold, and done in delicate silk, with fine antiques everywhere, and a chandelier which sparkled over them. The lights were down and there were candles burning on a table with a platter of cheese and fruit and a bottle of champagne chilling in a silver bucket.

Liz looked over at him with a smile, bereft of words at first. He did everything with such style and he was always so thoughtful. 'You're amazing, Mr. Fine... do you know that?'...

Sensuous and exciting. . . a romantic night of love, with the trappings of luxury and beauty. Two people breathing one another into themselves, their words, their actions, their physical surroundings all making up an atmosphere of love and excitement. It is romance vividly portrayed and deliciously experienced.

And when the inevitable sad moments come in the story, they, too, will be oversized and deeply affecting. In this case there will be terminal disease and an emotionally roiling custody battle where the outcome will never be certain until the very end. Characters cry, characters suffer, characters survive.

In romance fiction, atmosphere and mood are portrayed through sturdy emotion and sensuous surroundings. Think vividly, imagine high drama, write strongly.

The more explosive the romance, the more exciting the story.

And readers will applaud.

There are, to be sure, many, many other categories of fiction, and each one requires an emphasis on its special peculiarities in order to work. For example, a few years ago Roy Sorrels and Megan Daniel wrote:

> The spy-thriller addict loves colorful descriptions of great European capitals, written from the point of view of one who knows his way around and doesn't have to rely on [a] tour guide. . . Police procedural fans are hooked on the ambience, the bustle and activity of a precinct house and the sights of a world seen through the grimy windows of a patrol car. In Regency romances the story *must* take place in a world of richly furnished houses, elegant balls, shopping expeditions to chic shops, carriage rides etc. . .

On and on the special characteristics of each category can go. . . but there is one point above all to understand:
the reader must feel what the characters feel.

When that happens, we have the proper atmosphere and the proper mood for the story. Individual words and phrases, descriptive details or lack of them, particular settings and vivid emotional responses are the keys.

The reader must feel what the characters feel.

13

Conflict/Harmony

Once, a student of mine started a story this way:

Lightning flashed through the sky, while thunder rolled across the darkness and rain pelted down in great gobs. The wind howled its fury against the white clapboard house at the edge of the forest, drowning out sounds that might seep from the structure.

"I hate you talking to me like that!"

"Next time you better listen."

"You are a horrible man."

"Just like your mother. . ."

I reread it a couple of times sensing a problem but unable to pinpoint it. I put it down for a bit, then read it again. Now I saw.

The student had followed story-writing technique well. He had developed his sense of conflict right away, and he had

125

drawn it out sufficiently to grab the reader's attention. After all, a heavy storm raging about a lonely house at the edge of a forest is the stuff of suspense, mystery, horror, gothic, and the reader's sense of anticipation should take it from there.

But. . . my student overstepped himself when he portrayed the argument inside the house *in the midst* of the furious storm outside. If he wanted to show conflict, the storm itself would have been enough, *or* the argument inside the house would have done it. He didn't need both, and by using both he threw his entire opening out of balance.

Why?

Call it overkill, I suppose, but there is simply more evidence of conflict than the occasion calls for, and the result has to turn the reader off. Even though conflict is so important to all forms of story writing, it still requires a delicate touch to be most effective, and the mood we want to portray has to intrigue the reader and not desensitize him/her. "Never have the storm outside when there is a storm within," says novelist Sumner Locke Elliot, and how true that is! Keep the conflict localized; don't spread it around.

In my student's story, the mood of anger was portrayed inside as well as outside the house, and there wasn't much purpose in doing it this way. The mood could have been perceived in either instance, and the reader would have been spared a dose of overkill.

This doesn't mean, however, that in some instances similarity—or harmony—of mood and atmosphere can't be portrayed in two or three simultaneous circumstances. This is especially true when the mood or atmosphere is not crucial. . . as where the narrative relates a series of facts, such as in an historical episode, or dwells on analytical problem-solving. In either case, what mood the narrative depicts and what mood prevails can be similar because it isn't the mood that is so important; rather, it is the circumstances of the narrative that are key.

For example, a narrator could tell a story of treachery where anger and dishonesty flair, while in the very room as the narrator speaks, the overriding emotion—the mood and atmosphere—is also anger. The important thing is what happened, not who felt what.

Usually, however, writers tend to develop conflicts in their portrayals of mood and atmosphere for the simple, yet vital, reason that it makes things more interesting and more dramatic. Take this scene from Leo Tolstoi's *War and Peace,* and note the contrast between the battlefield carnage and the pre-battle serenity:

> Several tens of thousands of the slain lay in diverse postures and various uniforms. . . Over the whole field, previously so gaily beautiful with the glitter of bayonets and cloudlets of smoke in the morning sun, there now spread a mist of damp and smoke and a strange acid smell of saltpeter and blood. Clouds gathered and drops of rain began to fall on the dead and wounded, on the frightened, exhausted and hesitating men, as if to say, "Enough, men! Enough! Cease. . . bethink yourselves! What are you doing!". . .

Does not the very contrast add vividness to the mood of horror and death? If, a moment before battle, there could be gay beauty, glittering bayonets and cloudlets in the morning sun, doesn't the shattering of that image make the scene which follows it all the more impressive? It's as if we spill a bottle of black ink on a pure white carpet. . . the stain steps right out and confronts us. If the carpet had been a darker color, the stain would not have been so impressive.

But the sharper the contrast, the more significant the impression. In Tolstoi's epic, it was a case of playing the atmosphere of the physical world (the pre-battle serenity) against the mood of the characters (soldiers ready to kill one another). This is a useful technique and a powerful one, too. Anyone can do it! Watch:

— a character bubbling over with joy comes upon a severe auto accident
— in an atmosphere of suspicion one character has serenity
— in a Buddist monastery one character has murderous designs
— in a super-charged business meeting, one character dreams of his family's vacation

The notion of using conflict in mood and atmosphere follows the idea that readers want to be entertained, and this, in turn, is based upon the fact that underneath it all writers are storytellers.

Storytellers, first!

We use the technique of conflict to add drama to our words, to create a springboard for emotion. It is this emotion-charging that we hope will touch our audience. If they are touched by it, we add substance to the question *Where Are We?*—and to its answer...

Here, in this place, with this mood and this atmosphere.

See how Robert Coover uses conflict between the atmosphere of the physical surroundings and the mood of his characters in *The Gingerbread House,* a story of childhood innocence. Note how with just a couple of well-chosen adjectives he can develop his conflict:

A pine forest in the midafternoon. Two children

follow an old man, dropping bread crumbs, singing nursery tunes. Dense earthy greens seep into the darkening distance, flecked and streaked with filtered sunlight. Spots of red, violet, pale blue, gold, burnt orange. The girl carries a basket for gathering flowers. The boy is occupied with the crumbs. Their song tells of God's care for little ones. . .

The contrast is quite vivid, nothing subtle or hidden. It is the mixing of childhood innocence and the sinister pine forest, of serenity and evil. Note how Coover portrays the innocence of the two children: they drop bread crumbs, sing nursery tunes, the girl carries a basket, she seeks to gather flowers. Even following the old man seems innocent enough, and the colors of the filtered sunlight are happy, too: red, violet, pale blue, gold, burnt orange. . . these don't present an evil side. (Try gray, black, amber; these have a more sinister effect.)

But then look at his adjectives as he describes the pine forest: dense, earthy greens. . . darkening. . . flecked and streaked...These along with the time of day—midafternoon—leave us with the feeling that something sinister will happen. If it is a dense pine forest, we know from experience (and we remember the nursery rhymes from our youth) that the light will slowly recede and that the forest will grow ever more uncertain; something bad is bound to happen there!

The forest is a sinister place; those poor, innocent children are walking into trouble.

And what of the old man? Is he leading them into danger?

This is the atmosphere that the innocence of the children is in conflict with. The mood of innocence and the atmosphere of danger.

Doesn't it make a powerful coupling?

"Most successful atmospheric fiction," writes a current novelist, "achieves a balance of passion and detachment. Conrad's sea is beautiful and dangerous; Hemingway's Spain is violent and lovely. . ."

And Robert Coover's pine forests are serene and sinister.

Sometimes it is possible to have both conflict and harmony within the same small scene. The purpose would be to add vividness *and* to give substance to what is being portrayed. Conflict provides the emotion and the drama while harmony of mood and atmosphere provides dimension for the action to take place. For example, we could have a character in the depths of depression while moving through the lushness and beauty of a rain forest; suddenly the mood lifts, and the depression becomes manageable and a light touch of euphoria arrives. The mood of the character changes and slides into harmony with the fecund surroundings. The result is to give the new mood greater substance because it *fits* with the lush, beautiful atmosphere.

Marilyn French does this in a passage from her novel *The Bleeding Heart,* a story about an American woman in England who yearns for a permanent love relationship. One day she is on a train leaving London:

> . . . there would be warehouses and factories, sooty row houses, but each with a garden, and each garden held roses. Then suddenly, canals and the river, trees, horses, cows grazing under huge metal power poles. Sometimes a small barge on a canal, which would always make her lean forward, yearn toward it like a plant towards sun. She wanted to be sitting on the deck as the barge slid along the smooth waters, and try to catch sight of small game in the fields, to name the wild flowers. She wanted to be sitting there plump

in a heavy, holey sweater saying to the stocky bargeman, "Would you like a cup of tea, luv?" and watch him turn and smile, showing a few gaps in his uppers, and say "I would, old girl." The sex between them still alive despite the years, their pillowed bodies, hair grey and whispy in the light wind.

A dream. He drinks, she nags. . .

At first we get harmony of the physical atmosphere and the character's mood: the charming countryside (even the sooty row houses have rose gardens) with trees, cows grazing, canals and the river; the settled dream of marital bliss, mellow, fruitful, stable. . .

Then the last line: *he drinks, she nags.* A sudden conflict as the character's mood changes to a less pleasant reality. The charming countryside is still there, the barge still moves along the canal, the small game remains in the fields, the wild flowers are still there to be named, but now there is conflict between the character's mood and the physical atmosphere. She nags (call it anger), he drinks (call it frustration or unhappiness), and we have a blot on the happy, harmonious scene of a moment before.

But the change in mood from harmony to conflict actually heightens our interest in the story because it presents us with a vivid emotional contrast; now we understand the character's cynicism about the opposite sex, and now we appreciate why she could let herself dream about the pastoral scene—it is something she yearns for in spite of her cynicism.

What this does is give us insight into the character beyond a superficial emotional level; now we know what she *really* wants, and this means we come to understand her motivations. Because she can be both in harmony and in conflict with the physical atmosphere, we come to understand her at a deeper level.

Where are we?

On a train through the charming English countryside, dreaming of romantic love but aware that it could never be.

Harmony and conflict, they serve to emphasize both mood and atmosphere.

14

Mood and Atmosphere As Influenced by Physical Description

It is twilight, and a man sits quietly in his horse-drawn buggy in the middle of a street in the middle of a large city. Neither he nor his horse appears to move, even as thick, heavy snow covers them. They are like statues. . .

Do we have enough to develop an atmosphere, to create a mood? Do we need more description? Do these three sentences convey a sense of what the man must be feeling?

We could stretch a bit and say that the scene, from these three sentences alone, portrays a tableau, a still life of uninvolvement. . . perhaps. But that doesn't tell us much in terms of mood and atmosphere because we don't know the emotional make-up of the man, and we can't tell what is affecting him.

In short, we don't know—yet—how he fits in his own environment. In the hands of a skillful writer, however, things

133

would be different.

How's this:

> Large flakes of wet snow are circling lazily about the street lamps which have just been lighted, settling in a thin soft layer on roofs, horses' backs, people's shoulders, caps. Ione Patapov, the cabby, is all white as a ghost. As hunched as a living body can be, he sits on the box without stirring. If a whole snowdrift were to fall on him, even then, perhaps he would not find it necessary to shake it off. His nag, too is white and motionless. Her immobility, the angularity of her shape, and the sticklike straightness of her legs make her look like a penny gingerbread horse. . .

Now do we get a feeling for the mood and atmosphere? There's deadness here, isn't there? No spark, no life.

How do we know? Because we can sense the emotions of the cabby, and we see he does not care even if he were buried in the snow. He is a living deadman (the author describes him as "white as a ghost"), and this sets the mood and atmosphere.

The story is *Heartache* by Anton Chekov, and it is a classic example of how physical description can help to develop mood and atmosphere. Could we sense the cabby's despair if the weather was not so cooperative? Note how the cabby's emotions are emphasized by the weather. . . the heavy wet snow acts as a blanket on everything, it cakes the cabby, his horse and the surroundings into immobility, and this fits with the cabby's mood.

Why? Because a little later on we'll find out the cabby's only son died and there is no one but the cabby to mourn him, no one even to offer condolences.

Chekov sets it all up by having the physical environment

produce the deadness the cabby projects. See the individual elements he portrays:

— large wet snowflakes settling in a layer over roofs, horses, people
— the cabby is white as a ghost
— the cabby sits on the box without stirring
— the horse is white and motionless
— the horse looks like a piece of gingerbread

When all of this comes together, we have a portrayal of lifelessness, and that is precisely the author's intent. The mood and atmosphere is the product of this portrayal, and from it Chekov can develop the other elements of his story— theme, detailed characterizations, plot and so forth—against the background of this mood and atmosphere.

But could Chekov have accomplished the same thing without the physical description? Could he have portrayed the deadness as smoothly?

It would have been difficult without extensive narrative and/or further character development. I suppose he could have simply written "Ione Patapov is filled with despair because his only son has died and there is no one to mourn him," but this clearly lacks drama, and it doesn't grab the reader as neatly.

That's the point with using physical description to influence mood and atmosphere. It *adds* to the emotional build-up, and it envelops the reader in the story.

Mood and atmosphere become more vibrant this way, too.

Why characters do the things they do is often explainable by the mood and atmosphere they find themselves involved in. For example, an atmosphere of emotional liberation might cause people to act with animal instinct. . . or an atmosphere of total control might cause a character to develop a rich fantasy life. . . or an atmosphere of crass materialism might cause some to be cruel and inhumane to others. . .

Such moods and atmospheres can be helped by a dose of physical description which, in turn, can be the basis for characters to act in significant ways. Let's look at Leonard Michael's *The Men's Club,* for instance, the story of some men who meet because their women have extolled their own consciousness-raising group. As the evening progresses, the men grow more and more uninhibited until the host brings out a tray of throwing knives and the men take turns whipping the knives around the room marking up door, ceiling and walls. Then, Cavanaugh, one of the men, announces he used to play semi-pro baseball and after each game won the team members would howl like wolves because that was their nickname:

"Neat," said Canterbury. A white smile cut the gloomy face neatly. He tipped his head back, stretching the slender pipe of his neck and howled as if yearning after Cavanaugh's howl, catching its final note winding it highter, higher and higher toward sublimity. Berliner with lunatic enthusiasm came wailing after Canterbury. The three of them were howling together. Terry joined with a bellowing howl and then Paul started yipping hysterically. Now all five were doing it, harmoniously overlapping, layering the air with howls...

The physical description of the howling is really the effect of an atmosphere of emotional liberation. Why, after all, would a group of sane men act like animals unless their moods were spurred by some stimulus? In this case the stimulus is the gradual unburdening that comes from talking about themselves to the others, and as this occurs, the sense of liberation sets in. They feel freer, more open. . . so why wouldn't they howl like a bunch of wolves, why wouldn't they throw knives at the door, the ceiling, the walls?

They are, after all, liberated.

And the description of their howling and knife throwing gives us a concrete image of their sense of liberation. It influences the mood and atmosphere we feel.

When we speak of physical description, among the most obvious places to concentrate on is nature or weather or the general out-of-doors. These are so much around us that most writers find it hard to avoid introducing something about them in the majority of scenes. There is some purpose to this because such physical descriptions immediately give writer and reader a grounding in the familiar. We all know something about the weather, about nature and what we encounter outside our doors. It's often easier to describe these conditions than to dwell on the unfamiliar or the just-learned (for example, wouldn't it be simpler to describe a grove of recently picked apple trees than to describe the picking process itself?)

The point is really one we all know: the familiar is easier to describe and it comes off better.

But. . . there are subtleties to describing even those things we know well, and the influence of these physical descriptions can operate in surprising ways. Here's what Leonard Lutwack says in his book *The Role of Place in Literature:*

Atmospheric conditions of light and weather figure significantly in the tonality of out-of-door places. Night, rain, fog, sunlight change our perception of places. . . Uncontrollable natural events, such as storms, earthquakes and floods transform civilized functioning environments into places full of chaos and horror. Snow leaves a city intact but strangely without motion, static. . .

These elements of nature are all about us, and our tendency is to take them for granted. Yet they can be a useful technique for mood creation, and by describing them *with a purpose* we can enhance an already existing mood or even create one from scratch.

For example:

It was a fog that seemed to burst from the ocean floor, covering us in steamy nothingness as we entered the forbidden straits. It appeared as if ordered, fuzzy gray, fish-smelling, thick-coated. . . like an unfriendly tunnel. All visible signs had vaporized, shoreline, sun, clouds. . .

The mood is one of suspense and disorientation, and the fog helps to establish that. The more we describe the fog, its denseness, its sinister effects, the more we build the mood and develop the atmosphere. We could have written. . . "fog spread over us, and suddenly we couldn't see anything!" But this doesn't carry the drama that a full-fledged description of the fog would provide—"burst from the ocean floor"; "steamy nothingness", "fuzzy gray, fish-smelling, thick-coated." The more physical description we offer, the more influence that description will have on the mood and atmosphere. If we want to develop suspense and disorientation, the more sinister we make the fog the easier our task will be.

And we make the fog more sinister by adept physical description.

The same thing applies when we want to show character development. As we utilize physical description, this can have an effect on one or more characters, influencing—even con-

138

trolling—their mood or the general atmosphere. It's especially useful when we do it with nature or weather because the stronger we make our descriptions, the more significant their effect on the characters' moods.

See, for example, a story by O'Henry, *A Matter of Mean Elevation* in which Mademoiselle Giraud, an opera singer, has been performing with a travelling troupe in Venezuela. One day she is kidnapped by a band of Indians who live high in the Andes, and six months later, an American named Armstrong comes upon her—now treated like a princess by the Indians—and rescues her. As they begin their descent to sea level, she removes a leopard-skin robe because it is getting warmer.

> It seemed a trifle incongruous now. In the mountains it had appeared fitting and natural. And if Armstrong was not mistaken, she laid aside with it something of the high dignity of her demeanor. As the country became more populous and significant of comfortable life he saw, with a feeling of joy, that the exalted princess and priestess of the Andean peaks was changing to a women—an earth woman, but no less enticing. A little color crept to the surface of her marble cheek. She arranged the conventional dress that the removal of the robe now disclosed with the solicitous touch of one who is conscious of the eyes of others. She smoothed the careless sweep of her hair. A mundane interest, long latent in the chilling atmosphere of the ascetic peaks, showed in her eyes. . .

The closer they get to sea level the more earthy and crass she becomes, losing the goddess-like demeanor she showed while in the mountains, until finally she becomes the pragmatic performer, now vulgar and gross.

It is her mood that is changing in this story, and the mood changes as the scenery changes. In the mountains she was closer to the stars and away from earthly pursuits. . . so she acted like a goddess; at sea level she was closer to the center of the earth. . . so she acted like a flesh peddlar.

In this story the physical description controlled the mood of the character, and without such description there simply would not have been a story. The physical environment—and our use of it in our stories—plays a key role in how we want to set up mood and atmosphere. As we describe a scene, remember this:

THINK!

— do we want it to affect mood and atmosphere? If so, then:

— what mood and atmosphere do we develop?

— should the physical description control or simply influence the mood and atmosphere?

— what items in our physical description are best suited to develop mood and atmosphere?

Take a deep breath, arrange thoughts and. . .

Plunge in!

15

Mood and Atmosphere As Influenced
By The Five Senses

"Suppose we want to reflect a character's mood," I ask my writing class, "Where do we turn, first?"

"What the character says."

"What other characters say."

"What the author says."

"The author?" I ask. "You mean narrative?"

"It's either dialogue or narrative," a student answers. "One or the other."

"Maybe," I say. "What if the character can't speak?"

"The author describes the mood. It's narrative."

"He tells us, then?"

"Sure. . ."

" 'The character felt happy'. . . 'The character felt insecure'. . . something like that?"

"We know the character's mood, all right."

From the back of the room, a small voice. "We aren't showing it, though."

"What's wrong with narrative?" the first student asks.

"Even narrative can show us a character's mood." The small voice again. "It's *what* we have in the narrative that's important."

I nod. . . they're learning. . .

Dialogue to reflect a character's mood is easy. Sadness, anger, joy, terror. . . these things are portrayed in the words the characters use with one another. If it's sadness. . . "I break out and cry all the time, what's wrong with me?" If it's joy. . . "My God! What a wonderful evening. I won't be able to sleep for hours!"

With narrative it's a bit trickier. We can, of course, tell the reader what the character's mood is—joy, terror, gloom—and be done with it. But the careful writer will always think in dramatic terms and realize that the reader must have an image in her or his mind to complete the picture of what the words on the page intend. For example, if we wish to portray a gloomy mood, simply writing "this character feels gloomy" doesn't do much to develop a picture in the reader's mind. But we can fulfill that intention quite easily if we describe something *about* that character that will convey the gloominess.

How about. . . "He could see shades of gray in the wallpaper, dull, lifeless gray shades, and it could give him no further remorse. . ."

Or. . . "The odor of sour smoke hovered over the lifeless pile. He could taste nothing but the bitter aftereffects of death and sorrow. . ."

Many years ago a writer remarked, "The fiction writer can. . . reflect the mood of his character in a number of ways. He has recourse to all the five senses; unlike the dramatist, he can appeal to the senses of smell and taste and touch in addition to sight and sound.''

This is the way we have our narrative show a character's mood, *or* a general atmosphere. The five senses, using them to mold an image in the reader's mind. Try the following passage from Edgar Allan Poe's *The Fall of the House of Usher*. This is the opening of the story and note how the narrator's mood and the general atmosphere are established immediately through an appeal to the senses:

> During the whole of a dull, dark, and soundless day in the autumn of the year, when the clouds being oppressively low in the heavens, I had been passing alone, on horseback, through a singularly dreary tract of country, and at length found myself, as the shades of evening drew on, within view of the melancholy House of Usher. I know not how it was—but, with the first glimpse of the building, a sense of insufferable gloom pervaded my spirit...I looked upon the scene before me—upon the bleak walls—upon the vacant eye-like windows—upon a few rank sedges—and upon a few white trunks of decayed trees—with an utter depression of soul...

The sensory appeal here is mainly to what the narrator sees, but note the words and phrases that bring the sense of gloom right into the reader's mind:

— dull, dark and soundless day
— autumn of the year
— clouds being oppressively low in the heavens
— a singularly dreary tract of the country
— the melancholy House of Usher
— sense of insufferable gloom pervaded my spirit

— upon the bleak walls
— upon the vacant eye-like windows
— white trunks of decayed trees
— utter depression of soul

All of this in the opening paragraph of the story! A sense of gloom and decay fills the air, and we have no choice but to get caught up. See the adjectives he uses: *dull, dark, soundless, dreary, melancholy, insufferable, bleak, vacant, eye-like, decayed*. . . these paint the scene clearly and provide the gloomy atmosphere for the gloomy mood of the narrator. The appeal may be to only one of the five senses—sight—but it is so overwhelming as to carry off the entire scene without any added help.

Suppose, however, we wanted to add some other sensory perceptions to this same scene?

What about smell? "The acrid odor of decay rose up about me. . ."

Or touch? "Dead branches and leaves filled the forest floor. Each step brought the crunch of further detritus. . ."

Or taste? "My throat rebelled at the sharp, mildewed air that cascaded through my nostrils. . ."

No matter which of the senses is used, an air of drama will arise when we develop that word-picture for the reader. We must think images, and we use each of the senses to help us do that. Simply put, it is more effective if we allow the characters to perceive their own mood and atmosphere than if we—the writer—do it for them

Perhaps the most effective way to accomplish this is to develop a conflict between the characters and their atmosphere. For conflict read. . . resistance. . . that is, the characters strive to *resist* the atmosphere they are in.

—if the atmosphere is terror-filled, the characters

refuse to become terrified
— if the atmosphere is sunny and optimistic, the
    characters refuse to become sunny and optimistic
How do we portray this? By reference to the characters'
moods. And we do this by reference to the senses. . .
— Even though he smelled the sour fear of his com-
    rades and heard their hurried, panicky breathing,
    he would not allow himself to think of failure. He
    would survive, he would win. . .
— The soft breeze wound around without softening
    her air of gloom; the singing birds could not
    penetrate her closed-off hearing; the odor of
    frangipani dissolved before her pinched
    nostrils. . .
In the first example, we use the senses of smell and hearing
to convey the fear-laden atmosphere, and we have the
character—in contrast—refuse to buckle. In the second example, we use the senses of touch, hearing and smell to show
the balmy atmosphere, and we have the character—in contrast—refuse to be moved.

Resistance.

See how Elmore Leonard handles it with his novel, *Ban-
dits*. Jack Delaney used to do some burglary, but he hasn't in
quite a while. Now he finds he must do it again, this time in
—he hopes—an empty hotel room occupied by nasty Latins.
Note the contrast between the intimate room details and
Delaney's unsettled mood:

There was the bottle of wine Little One had delivered,
open in a silver bucket. A bowl of melted ice and
shrimp tails. Shrimp tails in ashtrays. Letters on the
desk by the TV set, the same letters he saw the last
time he was here.

Two packages of clean laundry on the bed. That could mean something. The light on in the bathroom. Towels on the floor. A bottle of cologne with the top off, on the washbasin. Next to it a blow-dryer, the cord plugged into the wall. He didn't want to be here.

He didn't want to be here the other night when he came. But this time the urge to hurry up and get out was stronger, the feeling more intense that he was crazy to be doing this. He was too old to be doing this. He wasn't the same person. He could feel it walking over to the dresser, his body telling him he shouldn't be here. He felt slow. . .

Delaney's unsettled mood is in his mind, he feels unsure of himself, and this communicates a general atmosphere of tension—will he succeed or won't he? Will he get out of the room without being caught? He *feels* his body not reacting as it should, and this, of course, is more akin to the sense of touch than anything else. Before this, however, Leonard goes into strong detail, giving us intimate glimpses into the character of those who occupied the room—open bottle of wine. . .shrimp tails in the ashtray. . .clean laundry on the bed. . . light on in the bathroom. . . towels on the floor. . . cologne bottle with the cap off. . . blow-dryer plugged in. . .

The intimate details of hotel-room living. Home-like, comfortable, unwary.

Then there's Delaney's mood—uncertainty. The opposite of what the room portrays.

Resistance.

The novelist G. Masterton gives us an excellent hint for using our senses to develop both a character's mood and a scene's atmosphere. "When it comes to people," he says, "I try not only to picture them but to imagine what they *sound* like, what they *smell* like, how they act. What they *feel* like too."

It's one thing to write that one character could smell body odor on another. . . but to get the most out of such a portrayal, shouldn't we put ourselves in the place of that odor-sensitive character, and see if we, too, can smell that body odor?

Whew!

Think reality, think images. It isn't enough to be one step removed. We—and our readers—must be part of the scene, we must live what is happening on the page.

Otherwise, our senses will close down, and we'll have nothing but the resources of a mummy when we try to explain the effects of mood and atmosphere.

Mummies, as we know, feel nothing.

16

Mood and Atmosphere As Influenced by Point of View

Remember the scene from Miguel Cervantes' *Don Quixote de la Mancha* when the knight errant and his faithful Sancho Panza come face to face with immobile, lifeless objects on the Plain of Montiel?

To Don Quixote they are wicked, threatening giants. . .

To Sancho Panza they don't look like giants, but if his master thinks they are, then. . .

To spectators and other minor characters they are windmills. . .

To us, the readers, they offer drama because they present us with choices depending upon the perceptions of the characters. They make us imagine and understand.

It is the point of view that we seize upon, and in doing this we realize that the mood and atmosphere shift with each perception.

Threat.
Watchfulness.
Ridicule.
Point of view. It will influence how the story proceeds and what the characters feel. To Don Quixote the threat brings an air (a mood) of conflict, and we are caught up in that at once; to Sancho Panza the watchfulness brings a touch of doubt yet it is more a case of following the call of duty; to the spectators and other minor characters it is simple foolishness, and they see only an old man in a suit of armor, astride a spavined old horse, tilting his lance and charging figments of his demented imagination.

But the point of view of each set of characters changes the mood of the story, and as we shift from one mood to another, we find our perceptions changing, too. No longer is it simply an old man doing a foolish thing, no longer is it a skeptical man servant shaking his head with doubt.

We come to understand! The mood-shifts give us substance and dimension, and the story develops as art.

Marjorie Mueller Freer suggests we stroll around a room and look at things from five different viewpoints—our own and four others, one of which should be as a character who has lived in the past. In effect we walk around the room in five different pairs of shoes, and if we do this, we. . . "come away with five varying views of the same room."

Five different points of view. For example:
- one character might spy a snuff box stolen from his father's home twenty years before
- another character might relish the large onamented windows and recall the pleasures of his grandfather's sunlit library when he was a child

— a third character might note the eclectic furnishings and be confirmed in her view that the host and hostess have poor taste

Note the moods developed by these differing viewpoints:

— suspicion
— wistfulness
— disdain

The same details seen differently by different characters. Their points of view will set up the mood and atmosphere of the scene.

There is a technique to all of this, and it's based on a simple principle. For William Sloane it's a question of "who, from the reader's point of view, is telling the story." Is it the narrator, in which case it becomes an "I" story, a first-person story? Is it "a central character who is told about by the writer, but as if the writer were serving for the reader"? Is it "a series of characters, each of whom, in turn, perceives for the reader"? Or is it "a never-named and omniscient narrator"?

We write our stories from a certain point of view, and the accomplished writer knows that the choice of point of view will control style (type of speech, diction, long or short sentences and so forth) and story progress. So the choice should be made ahead of time, and among the choices are these:

— first person *(I see a rainbow)*
— third person subjective *(Was that a rainbow, she asked herself?)*
— third person objective *(He sees a rainbow)*
— omniscient *(A rainbow appeared before him)*

There are other narrower categories that writers have used through the centuries, and are still using, but the ones above are the basic approaches, and it is through one or more of these that the great bulk of literature thrives. In general terms, the differences between the points of view are more a question of how challenging the writer wants to be to himself/herself and to the reader. With first person, for example, the writer is limited to perceptions of that character because the entire story is told through one person's eyes. This might work well with mystery-suspense stories, but it has drawbacks in other kinds of fiction. With third person subjective, we can get into the character's mind, and this type of approach allows us to grow more intimate with the character. Not only do we see what he sees, but we know what he thinks, too.

Third person objective, however, is more limiting. Now we are like a camera, and we see only what the camera can focus upon. . . He sees and sees and sees, but we don't know what he thinks or feels. This technique works best with short fiction because it is so unvarying that it would drag after a while.

The omniscient approach allows us to play God, to be everywhere, to know everything. It is the least limiting of the techniques and it provides us an opportunity to move from character to character, event to event without struggling to stay within narrow boundaries—unless we wish to do so for the sake of the story, as when we allow the reader to receive certain information we deliberately make inaccessible to one or more characters.

For our purposes the importance of understanding these points of view is to recognize that they can be used to create a mood or atmosphere. For example, with the first-person approach, a mood of suspense can be created quite readily:

I wondered at the chipped window frame even as I

lowered myself into the room. The darkness magnified every sound, but I couldn't help scraping the edge of the frame with my fingernail. A residue of white seemed to catch on it, and I had a quick thought it might—just might—come from the newly painted carrying case with the sculpture inside. . .

The first-person approach allows us to use both subjective and objective techniques, but try and stretch this over book length, and it becomes more difficult. Unless the narrator is a riveting personality, the story will tend to slow down. . .

Unless we go to multiple points of view. Try this passage from Jessamyn West's *The Massacre at Fall Creek*. It is a story of an Indian massacre in 1824, and the subsequent trial of two men for the crime. Caleb Cope is an outstanding citizen of the local town, though he has witnessed an incriminating statement by Luther Bemis who is one of the accused. It is the opening day of the trial and both Caleb and Luther are in the courtroom, sitting next to one another:

It was a mild day, and the heat of all those bodies packed into a space too small for them had raised the room's temperature to that of midsummer. It was the smell of nervousness and fear, of curiosity and cruelty, with a strong whiff added of winter underwear not shed since last November.

He reached over, put a hand on Luther Bemis's. . .

Lute knew what that meant. Armitage was about to call him to the stand, and Caleb was giving him comfort. Or would give him a shove with a hand, hard and splintery as a roof shake, if he saw any signs of faltering.

Lute wouldn't back down. . .

There are actually three points of view in this short passage

—omniscient, third person objective, third person subjective. The first paragraph is author—omniscient, and note
the mood—suspenseful, uncertain. The author tells us, and
we find out how people are feeling, what they are wearing,
even what they smell or smell like. Using sensory perceptions
like this provides the basis for the mood (smelling of nervousness and fear, of curiosity and cruelty), and the author
can roam where she likes in order to present it.

Then, in one short sentence, she changes the point of view.
"He reached over. . ." tells us what Caleb *does*, not what he
is thinking, and this, of course, is third person objective. Just
like a camera. What's the mood here? Comforting, perhaps.
Or maybe supportive. But clearly different from the atmosphere of suspense a moment before. Now we've not only
changed points of view, we've changed mood and atmosphere, too. Could the point of view have remained the
same even with the changed mood and atmosphere?

Try it and see. . . Does the omniscient point of view carry
the same impact in both instances?

Probably not. The simple act of touching another's hand is
more meaningful if it is described unadorned. The omniscient
approach would require more words, more narrative.

And it would lose something.

The final portion is third person subjective, and here again
the mood changes. Now we're in Lute's head, and we sense
his cynicism. He won't be comforted by Caleb's gesture, and
he knows what he must do. The mood is one of determination and self-confidence. Note how much more intimate we
can be with Lute than we could be with Caleb. Caleb patted
Lute's hand, and we can only guess at his motive. . . but with
Lute we *know* how he reacts, and what he intends to do. The
points of view change, the mood changes and so does the

focus of the story.

We should be careful, however, not to assume that mood and atmosphere will dictate the point of view we want to take. It's really the other way around, and once we've set our point of view, then we see what mood or atmosphere would fit. If it's first person, for example, we'd have to gauge how the mood and atmosphere could be portrayed, given the limitations of the first-person approach; that is, since everything is seen through the eyes of the narrator, the mood or atmosphere would have to develop from his or her viewpoint alone.

Or if it's third person subjective, we could have mood and atmosphere created in more intimate terms, though it would lose something because there would be little rapid exposition (He watched, He saw, He went, He took, He shot. . .). Things would develop more slowly, more cerebrally.

See, however, how an accomplished writer like Joan Didion handles a shifting point of view with rapid-fire prose. Note that all but the final sentence is in the first person, and that it is objective and camera-like. It's from her novel, *Democracy,* and the passage occurs right after word that a close friend of the narrator's has been shot:

I was trained to distrust other people's versions,
but we go with what we have.

We triangulate the coverage.

Handicap for bias.

Figure in leanings, predilections, the special circumstances which change the spectrum in which any given observer will see a situation.

Consider what filter is on the lens, so to speak. What follows is essentially through Billy Dillon's filter.

"This is a bitch," Billy Dillon remembered Dick
Ziegler saying over and over. . .

Two points of view. . . first person, and then briefly, third person subjective. Note the analytical style of the first person approach, the fact that the narrator can explore her method of observation and provide us with a sense of suspenseful foreshadowing. Her mood is dispassionate, yet in the understatement of her words we sense something dramatic. *I was trained to distrust other people's versions*. . . she begins, and with those words we know there will be some tension and uncertainty. The mood is clearly defined. . .

Until we get to Billy Dillon's remembrance. Then we're in another point of view as intimate, perhaps, as what precedes it, but different, too. It's no longer what the narrator feels, now it's what Billy Dillon remembers and feels. Still tension-laden, still dramatic (with anger or frustration added), but different.

What we have, then, is a shift of point of view. . . without a corresponding shift in mood and atmosphere. Same tension, same uncertainty, only now it's seen from two viewpoints. Does it make a difference?

Here's what Lawrence Block says: ". . .[multiple] viewpoint characters advance the plot, enlarge the book's scope, provide additional perspectives on the lead. . ."

Even though the mood and atmosphere don't change.

Think viewpoint, *first*!

Then fit in mood and atmosphere. It works, it really does.

17

Mood and Atmosphere

As Change of Pace

A few years ago I was asked to lecture at a well-known writer's conference. After the lecture I attended a faculty reception and found myself in a circle with two highly praised fiction writers. One of them was commenting on a student whose work he had just read.

"The talent's pretty raw, but he has a feeling for words."

"I have a couple like that," said the other writer.

"If only they understood what their talent can have them do! It's like they're steering in a vacuum."

"We'll teach 'em the right way, I guess."

"Look at this!" The first writer showed us the student's manuscript, and the opening three and one half pages were nothing but narrative. A lengthy exposition of sadness and gloom. "Too much, too much!" he said, "we're wallowing in it."

"A little dialogue wouldn't hurt in there," the second writer said.

"Pace," said the first writer, flipping through the manuscript pages. "This guy needs a lesson in pace."

Ah-ha, I thought. "Pace is a four-letter word meaning time," I said.

They both looked at me, then the first writer smiled. "Like in music," he said.

"Like in the beats to music," the second writer added. . .

Pace. Every story has pace, and the writer who ignores it will have a jumbled mess on his hands. The pace of any story is its beat, its relative movement, and for a story to work, the pace must be smooth and purposeful.

For example, a three and a half-page opening which creates gloom and sadness—all narrative—is overpaced, it goes on too long. One of the writers suggested breaking it up with dialogue, and that certainly would work because dialogue between narrative passages—or vice-versa—does change the pace.

But another technique would work, also. We change the mood or atmosphere, we break up the pace by creating something different. . .

So the reader won't get bogged down. If we cruise along at only one speed, eventually we'll lose that reader because he or she will get sucked into unbroken ennui. The effect of the drama will disappear.

But if we change that pace, the reader will be jarred enough so his or her attention won't flag.

"Pay attention!" the change of pace is saying. "Something new and different is about to happen."

Novelist Mary Stewart sees change of pace as similar to the curtain in the theatre. It works "to open a scene, or act as changeover points for emphasis and direction, either of action or emotion," she says. Descriptive passages "can break up a long dialogue or action sequence and provide points of rest; they can also allow the writer to slip essential information in among semi-relevant or purely atmospheric detail."

Certainly, mood and atmosphere can be created by descriptive passages and if descriptive passages can perform a change-of-pace function, then mood and atmosphere should be part of that, too. In effect, narrative with a new mood and atmosphere can provide a double-edged effect:

— the narrative, itself, acts to change the pace from the preceding sequence of dialogue or action
— the new mood and atmosphere is a change from the mood and atmosphere that preceded it

Let's look at an example. In Raymond Carver's story, *A Small, Good Thing,* Ann orders a birthday cake for her young son's birthday, but before the cake can be picked up, the son is in a terrible automobile accident and lingers for several days in the hospital, his parents at his side. From time to time the parents receive nasty phone calls from someone using their son's name, and after the boy dies, Ann figures it has to be the baker of the birthday cake which has never been picked up and paid for. Ann, and her husband Howard, filled with anger, go down to the bakery to confront the baker, but in the middle of the tense scene Ann breaks down and tells the baker the boy has died. The baker, who has been holding a rolling pin because of their belligerence, invites them to sit down.

"Forgive me, if you can," the baker said. "I'm not an evil man, I don't think. Not evil, like you said on the phone. You got to understand that what it comes down to is I don't know how to act anymore, it would seem. Please," the man said, "let me ask you if you can find it in your heart to forgive me?"

It was warm inside the bakery. In a minute Howard stood up from the table and took off his coat. He helped Ann from her coat. The baker looked at them for a minute and then nodded and got up from the table. He went to the ovens and turned off some switches. He found cups and poured coffee from an electric coffee maker. He put a carton of cream on the table, and a bowl of sugar. . .

Note how the atmosphere changes. . . When Ann and Howard first arrive at the bakery they are angry and hurt, their son has just died and all they can focus on is that another human being is deliberately causing them pain; the baker, too, is angry because he hasn't been paid for the birthday cake he made to order.

Then Ann breaks down. Now note the atmosphere shift, first with the passage of dialogue and then with the narrative. Suddenly there is kindness and thoughtfulness, repentance. The baker has a change of heart. . . and the story has a change of pace.

Ann and Howard, too. After the baker asks their forgiveness, they remove their coats, a signal that they want to feel comfortable. And so the baker pours everyone a cup of coffee.

What we have here is a clear change of pace through a change in the atmosphere (and in the moods of the characters, too). From belligerence to forgiveness, from hurt to healing, the story has moved forward. And see how the change of pace has helped:

— would the story be as poignant if Howard and Ann retained their anger?

— would the baker be as sympathetic if he had retained his meanness?

— does the narrative paragraph add substance to what each of the characters is feeling and saying?

Isn't the story better with this change of pace?

Of course it is.

There are times when a change of pace can occur right within the passage itself, when part of a passage follows one mood and then there is a shift. It is useful for the same reasons that a more general change of pace is useful—it avoids monotony, retains the reader's attention and gives the story substance.

For example:

One-by-one the family inched toward the dark wood casket, denuded of flowers now in preparation for the trip to the cemetery. The afternoon light was gray-filled, and as each family member bent over the casket, the thick sadness of the moment seemed blanketed by the ashes of the fading sun. Suddenly a radio sounded. . . not loud but compelling, somewhere outside, a disco beat, dah-dah-dah-dah-dah-dah-dah-dah. . . A few heads looked up, a few fingers tapped thighs, some toes moved in time. . .

"Oh my God!" It was Mama Francis, weeping and throwing herself over the coffin. . .

Within the same passage we go from a mood of sadness and gloom to a touch of pleasure and excitement and then back again to the sadness. But we do have the change of pace, and this gives the entire passage more impact. We don't lull the reader with a lengthy sameness of mood and atmosphere; instead, we offer change, and this kindles interest.

The point, of course, is to use mood and atmosphere as a

technique for developing the story, and when we change pace, we have a story with some dimension. See how Howard Fast does this same thing in his novel, *The Dinner Party*. It is the story of one day and evening in the home of a U.S. Senator from Virginia. The Senator's son and the son's friend, Jones, are home from law school, and the Senator's daughter, Elizabeth, is there, too. Jones, who is Black and from a poor southern family, and the Senator's son are invited up to Elizabeth's room before dinner:

Jones reacted strangely to Elizabeth's room. It was a large, beautiful room, with a fireplace piled with wood and framed in a white mantel, white woodwork, wallpaper of dusty rose toile, Portuguese grospoint rugs on the floor, framed eighteenth century fashion prints, and a portrait of her great-grandmother done by John Singer Sargent. On the bed was an ancient coverlet of stitched silk that some poor Italian woman of a century ago had dulled her eyesight to create. The windows were draped with starched organdy, and the painted electrified oil lamps went well with the old cherry-wood furniture. At first sight the room threw him off, and he was possessed with a feeling akin to panic. . .

At first sight the room threw him off, and he was possessed with a feeling akin to panic. . . this is the change of pace. All that goes before it is physical description that sets a tone of luxury and comfort, an atmosphere, really, of serenity.

But then comes panic. Jones feels panicky, even though he is in the middle of luxury. The mood changes, the atmosphere changes. . . suddenly!

The pace changes, as well. What had been a leisurely stroll through a finely furnished room now becomes—unexpectedly—a sharp intake of breath.

. . . *he was possessed with a feeling akin to panic.* . .

Panic!

No more leisurely stroll. The pace has changed.

And the reader's interest has been piqued, once again.

18

Using Nostalgia

It was the second week into the term, and my writing class had met but once. A student called me on the phone.

"I'm worried about the course," she said. "You told us to review our lives and come up with a story."

"An experience," I corrected. "Something you've lived through."

"I've thought about it and. . . well, there's nothing. I mean, my life's been pretty dull."

"What about your childhood?" I asked.

There was a sigh, a brief yearning. "Could we go back that far?"

"Whatever you've lived through."

"I remember the streetcars we took to school, and the games we used to play to see who could ride without paying. . . 'the girl in back has the change,' and we'd rush

165

out the door, laughing. . . of course the motorman would remember us, and he knew who had big brothers and sisters, he'd eventually tell them, and they would pay our fares. . ."

"Where was this?" I asked.

"Oh, Tasmania. . . you know, Australia . . ."

My life's been pretty dull. Exotic Tasmania, far-off Australia, the questions about growing up there abound. How many Americans have ever had such an experience, how many would be interested to know what it was like?

"I think you'll be surprised at the response you'll get," was all I could say.

Remembering our childhood or some other significant point in our lives is a way of providing depth to our own self-characterization. It gives to others further clues and information about who we are and where we came from. If we apply it as a technique in fiction, it means we can more fully develop a character or help to explain a storyline.

Remembering. . . we call this nostalgia. It is a yearning to return to some past period, a wistful hope to relive the pleasures of the past.

In terms of mood and atmosphere it means we use nostalgia to develop feelings and emotions that will help to characterize a basic scene we are producing. For example, if we wish to portray unsettled domestic life, we could have a character remember a time in his or her childhood when things seemed most settled and secure, when the world was in harmony and domestic life seemed blissful.

The nostalgia reference has two purposes: it can add substance to the basic mood by developing a contrast (such as the settled nostalgia, the unsettled present), and it can give us more information about a character or group of characters so we come to know them better and identify with them more easily.

In effect, using nostalgia allows us to develop our mood and atmosphere to the point where the past and the present operate together and produce a stronger emotional response, both from the characters in the story and from the readers, as well. Nostalgia gives us depth.

But nostalgia has to be managed properly. It "must be used only as background (and not go on for too long)" says novelist Sumner Locke Elliott. What he means is that when we write:

> I am walking to school among the mists that float
> over the newly harrowed fields, and I feel a sense of
> elation because the spring chores are done. I clutch
> my home-made swimsuit and savor the anticipation
> of the tingling water at the gorge. I can hear songbirds
> in the high trees, and I smile. I am nine years old. . .

we should only be providing background for the character who is doing the remembering. This nostalgia is to give us some additional insight into that character who is portrayed through the bulk of the story at a much older age. How old? That doesn't matter, so long as the passage of nostalgia (and keep in mind. . . it should not go on too long) is inserted into the story for purposes of *background*! Most of the story must deal with the character in the present, at an older age and under different circumstances than the passage of nostalgia offers.

What happens if we try to make nostalgia the basic story?

Two hundred and fifty pages of yearning and wistfulness, a storyline bathed in one stretched-out emotion. The plot would be thin, and the characterizations limited. The impact of the nostalgia would soon be lost.

That's why we keep it short and pointed.

See how Evelyn Waugh captures the sense of nostalgia while maintaining an effective storyline in his work, *Brideshead Revisted*. Charles, the narrator, is in the army and camped near Brideshead Castle, where he spent much of his youth. All of this information is provided in a prologue, and then the story opens:

"I have been here before," I said; I had been there before; first with Sebastian more than twenty years ago on a cloudless day in June, when the ditches were white with fool's parsley and meadow sweet and the air heavy with all the scents of summer; it was a day of peculiar splendour, such as our climate affords once or twice a year, when leaf and flower and bird and sun-lit stone and shadow seem all to proclaim the glory of God; and though I had been there so often, in so many moods, it was to that first visit that my heart returned on this, my latest. . .

A wistful memory, is it not? Note how Waugh uses nature to bring the memories flooding back. . . "cloudless day in June". . . "ditches were white with fool's parsley and meadow sweet". . . "air heavy with all the scents of summer". . . "when leaf and flower and bird and sun-lit stone and shadow". . . What these remembrances do is to create both a setting *and* a mood because they are not only telling us where we are but how we're feeling, too.

How is Charles feeling?

Wistful because the memories are good. And if the memories are good, then Charles, himself, twenty years later, must be in a pleasant frame of mind. Using nostalgia like this will set that mood, and the story can continue from that point.

Think of nostalgia as a technique, not unlike the use of

time (chapter ten) or the use of an appeal to one of the senses (chapter fifteen). The technique is utilized to portray mood and atmosphere in order to develop a more dramatic and a more substantial storyline. Nostalgia doesn't work in every instance—for example, in a tense confrontation, it would be ludicrous to have a character become nostalgic when his or her life may be on the line. On the other hand, when the situation calls for mellowness or pure joy, a bit of nostalgia might be the perfect key to effective portrayal of the mood and atmosphere.

One place nostalgia works well is in characterization. It can add to what we already know about the character doing the remembering, and it can provide us information about the people who are in the nostalgia scene. We could find out, for example, *why* someone does something. . .

— I was six years old and the crystal blue of the pond beckoned me for the first time. "Jump! I'll catch you," it said. I've never doubted that voice. . .

Or why someone *doesn't* do something. . .

— I remembered the little toad we found under a bush by the sand dunes when my parents had the big house on the island. "Crush 'im," Harry yelled, but I prevented his stomp. "He may have a family, somewhere," I said. . .

As we develop characterization through nostalgia, we add to mood and atmosphere by showing the emotions that are part of any scene. The more emotional content in the scene, the stronger the mood and atmosphere are, and this, then, will keep our readers locked to the page.

The bottom line. Readers reading what we write.

Try this characterization from nostalgia. In Richard Price's novel, *The Breaks,* the narrator remembers growing up in a housing complex in Yonkers, New York. A large grassy plot was the local ballfield, and there was a bench known as "the fathers' bench" where parents would watch their kids perform. One cold November morning as the kids prepared to play football:

Me and my friends were out on the grass field choosing up sides, the fathers were on their bench, when suddenly (WEE CHALLENGE!!) the fathers all rose and came stomping onto the field. It took us a second to catch on to what was happening, but when we did we went berserk. The fathers were gonna play us! Hot damn! But they were very self-conscious. I could see it in how they came marching onto the field; bumping into each other, laughing too easy, jingling the change in their pockets. . .

The football game goes on, and the narrator's father embarrasses him severely. But in this scene we come to understand the relationship between the narrator and his father, and this, in turn, allows us to know the narrator better. Mood and atmosphere turn on this nostalgic interplay, and we can sense why the narrator is angry or forlorn.

It's a simple equation:

— nostalgia gives us clues to characterization
— characterization gives us one basis for mood and atmosphere.

The truth is that nostalgia is capable of working in a variety of circumstances, and developing characterization is only one of them. In chapter fifteen we discussed how we appeal to sensory perceptions and how that can influence mood and atmosphere.. . .

The same sort of thing applies with nostalgia. Nostalgia can appeal to sensory perceptions—to our sight, smell, touch, taste and hearing—and the mood and atmosphere will be enhanced. A nostalgic reference is an appropriate vehicle for this because we are *seeking* something memorable, and when it registers on our senses, we won't forget it.

See how it works:

— Twenty years later the smell still tingles my nostrils. . .

— When I was six, the bells spoke their own beautiful language to me—they still do, twenty years later. . .

In his reminiscence, *The Last Time I Saw Paris,* Elliot Paul describes springtime in Paris during the 1920s:

In spring one would be aware of a fragrance or balm in the air, sharpened by gasoline fumes. Suddenly, on the way to lunch, one would see a small irresponsible dog rolling over a patch of sunshine. New leaves would appear on the plane-trees and horse-chestnuts. Turtles, pigeons, hens, canaries and love birds would be placed on the sidewalks in front of pet shops and feed stores. The first *bateau mouche* (small passenger steamers) would pass under a bridge with a load of shivering passengers. Café terraces would spread in area and show sudden animation. . .

Note the sensory appeal here. . . to our smell ("fragrance or balm in the air"), to our sight ("small irresponsible dog"), to our hearing ("canaries"). . . Don't we get the feel of Paris at this time? Isn't the mood one of pleasurable re-awakening? As he reminisces don't we find ourselves imagining the smells, the sights, the noises?

And isn't this exactly what nostalgia is supposed to do? If it is a wistful remembering, then how better to accomplish it than by tickling our sensory perceptions so they create sensory images we can enjoy?

Paris in the 1920s, springtime, a re-awakening.

Isn't that some nostalgia?

Hemingway, Fitzgerald, and a host of others would certainly agree.

19

The Importance of Tone

Suppose we're Lewis Carroll and we're doing a segment of *Alice's Adventures in Wonderland:*

"I'm sad," says Alice. "I think I'll write a sad story."

"Stories aren't sad," says the Red Queen, "only words are sad."

"No, no," the King of Hearts interrupts. "Sad is what you feel. Mad is what you feel. Sad, mad. . . stories can't cry, words can't sniffle. Poor things."

"Readers cry and sniffle," Alice says.

"I worry about words. Readers can take care of themselves," the Red Queen huffs. "What is a story but a bunch of words?"

"What's a bunch of words without a shepherd?" the King of Hearts points out. "Someone has to know where the next pasture is."

"The next *grassy* pasture, you mean," says Alice with confidence.

"The next *comfortable* pasture," the King of Hearts corrects. "A bunch of words won't do anything unless they're comfortable."

"What if it's a rainstorm or snowing?"

"Words have no problem with that."

"Is a rainstorm sad, is a snowstorm mad?"

The Red Queen shakes her head. "Words don't feel. Words do."

"Readers feel," says Alice.

"Words *make* readers feel," the Red Queen insists.

"Comfortable words make comfortable readers," the King of Hearts says. "Words must be comfortable. Everyone knows that. . ."

When we write, our words must do many things, and one of the most important is to develop a level of comfort so the reader isn't jarred or embarrassed by what he or she reads. I don't mean that our words shouldn't push readers into unsettled feelings—if that is our intention—because the comfort level, the writer's professional competence, is still there. But we must avoid stylistic awkwardness which will undo the comfort level we are seeking to maintain. In the passage above, the characters are talking about the comfort level of words and what it means. . . "Words *do*" says the Red Queen. . . "Readers *feel*" Alice answers. . .

This is the comfort equation. Words will create the comfort, and readers then absorb it. But it must be the words that come first, and we must understand that the underlying principle is this:

Consistency!

Say it aloud. . . Con. .sis. . .ten. .cy!. . . This is what comfort is all about, this is what style is all about, this is what makes readers feel.

Consistency!

It means not deviating from the general stylistic pattern set early in the story, it means maintaining a steady attitude and weaving it through the work. It means paying attention to the tone of the story. . .

Tone. This is what consistency influences, this is what every work has, and writers have to be aware that the tone they develop is the tone they *want* to develop. For example, if we wish to develop a sinister tone (such as Edgar Allan Poe or Stephen King might do), we would not want to minimize its effect by injecting too much explanation or avoiding words and phrases that might spark it. We would want to maintain a consistent, sinister tone.

And as we develop our tone, its basic impact is on mood and atmosphere. If our tone is sinister, certainly the mood and atmosphere would have to reflect that, and we could then use some of the techniques already mentioned to portray it— sensory images, for example, conflict and harmony choices, changing point of view, nostalgia and so forth.

The equation: *if consistency equals tone, tone equals mood and atmosphere*

That's why tone is important.

See how one writer puts it: "Part of the atmosphere is *tone*, an attitude taken by the narrative voice that can be described, not in terms of time and place, but as a quality— sinister, facetious, formal, solemn and so on. . ."

It is the quality—the style—of the words that is important. We seek a tone to our work and we develop mood and atmosphere from it.

Tone will take many forms, of course, but one of the most beautiful is when it's touched with poetry. . . the poetic tone, even with narrative. Here's something from William Faulkner's *The Hamlet*, the story of Frenchman's Bend, a small rural town. Mrs. Armstid, one of the characters, is looking over the town from the gallery of Varner's Store:

> After a time Mrs. Armstid raised her head and looked up the road where it went on, mild with spring dust, past Mrs. Littlejohn's, beginning to rise on past the not-yet-bloomed (that would be in June) locust grove across the way, on past the schoolhouse, the weathered roof of which, rising beyond an orchard of peach and pear trees, resembled a hive swarmed about by a cloud of pink-and-white bees, ascending, mounting toward the crest of the hill where the church stood among its sparse gleam of marble headstones in the sombre cedar grove where during the long afternoons of summer the constant mourning doves called back and forth. . .

Note the images:

—the road (mild with spring dust—past the not-yet-bloomed locust grove)

— the schoolhouse (weathered roof resembling a hive swarmed about by a cloud of pink-and-white bees)

— the church (among its sparse gleam of marble headstone—in the sombre cedar grove)

Read this aloud, and its poetic tone comes alive. It resonates with imagery and sensuous appeal, and it could easily be rearranged into poetic stanzas. The road is "mild with spring dust". . . there is an "orchard of peach and pear trees". . . the weathered roof looks like "a cloud of pink-and-white bees". . . the sombre cedar grove holds "the constant mourning doves [calling] back and forth". .

A series of clear images emerges in our minds, and we acquire a picture of the town. We can see it, hear it, smell it, feel it. It is poetic in the sense that Faulkner has used his words sparingly (one relatively short paragraph to describe an entire town), he has developed a comfortable rhythm (read this aloud, it has a definite beat), he has sprayed his text with images. . .

And he has maintained a consistent tone. It is poetic and it is familiar.

How do we maintain that consistency? By careful use of words and phrasing. If the tone is formal, stay away from the informal; it the tone is gloomy, stay away from happy or joyful comments; if the tone is fast paced, stay away from lengthy, analytical narratives; if the tone is studied and somber, stay away from snappy, action-packed scenes with a lot of mirth; if the tone is satire, avoid words and phrases that neutralize the circumstances or characteristics to be satirized.

The point is this: every story has—or should have—tone, and we must be aware of what it is, we must strive to keep it consistent and we must use it to develop our mood and atmosphere.

This is true even if the mood and atmosphere may change. The tone must remain steady and straight. See this selection from Francine Prose's book, *Household Saints*. Lino Falconetti has been playing pinocle with butcher Joseph Santangelo for a long time and losing and finally, one night, half in jest, he bets his daughter, Catherine, on a hand and loses again. Joseph holds him to the wager, even though Lino knows his daughter would never go along. But more to make peace than anything else he invites Joseph to have dinner with them, and he goes home and announces the invitation to

Catherine:

"I want this meal to be so good a man would get married to eat like that every night."

Suddenly Catherine remembered Joseph Santangelo telling her to ask her father where he could put his thumb. And now she understood what he'd meant as she imagined it, swollen to monstrous proportions, squashing the Falconettis like ants.

"I've got news for you," she said. "No one gets married for the food."

———

Catherine awoke at three in the morning with a vague sense of something wrong. She checked back over the previous day, imagined into tomorrow, got as far as Joseph Santangelo and stopped right there. By dawn she was in no shape to cook up a storm. Long before she started cooking, she knew that it was going to be one of those days when everything goes wrong in the kitchen. . .

Two scenes, back-to-back, two different moods, but a consistent tone. In the first scene the mood from Catherine's point of view is one of defiance. . . she remembers Joseph and his bullying manner, and she announces to her father that his motives for inviting Joseph aren't going to work. "No one," she says, "gets married for the food". . .

Meaning: it isn't going to work, this dinner invitation and what you hope it might accomplish. I don't like Joseph, my cooking isn't going to make a difference.

In the second scene, we have Catherine, no longer defiant, now simply unnerved. She has had a chance to reflect on what her father is trying to do, and while she doesn't like it any better, she now senses her own futility. Even if (a big if!)

she went along with her father's plan, the dinner would turn out poorly. Her anger is still there, only now it is directed more at herself than at Joseph. She is uncertain, unhappy and without confidence. The mood is one of minor panic, and we know how this can vibrate through a scene.

But look at the tone. Through two different moods, the tone doesn't change; it is straightforward if a bit understated, snappy and quick paced, informal and pleasantly dramatic. There is no shouting or screaming, no emotion-wracked confrontation, no lengthy narrative to explain feelings, no melodrama in the father-daughter relationship.

In a word, the tone remains. . . consistent!

If we think of tone as an element of style, it might be easier to understand. In simplest terms, style is "the way" something is presented, and tone, therefore, becomes its voice. A consistent tone is one safeguard to a consistent style, and this is crucial for attaining reader involvement. How effective would a story be if:

— it started out action-packed and withdrew into dreamy stream-of-consciousness after fifty pages?

— it wavered between tongue-in-cheek satire and vicious anger?

— it offered a solemn perspective but without arousing sympathy or empathy?

What tone does is to keep things on path and to set up a framework for mood and atmosphere. Style "speaks" through tone, and tone "speaks" through mood and atmosphere.

Consistency is the key.

Without it the door to mood and atmosphere remains locked.

20

The Nature of Nature

It is dusk on the beach, the end of a summer day, and the colors are changing. There are birds and several die-hard swimmers. . .

This is the basic scene, the essential elements. Suppose that out of these elements we want to create a mood of joy and contentment. Would we write:

— The setting sun bathing in the darkening sea, poured its purple gold rays into the sparkling azure depths. The pelicans soared and glided over the surface, graceful in soundless flight. . .

Or would we write:

— A simple bottle washed up, sparkling with red and orange and purple reflections. A small boy stopped to admire the kaleidescope before he. . .

Writing about nature is one of the most valuable tools we

have for developing mood and atmosphere. Nature can be personified, made into an actual character and provided with influence—even control—over the storyline. Nature can live!

And it can acquire a mood and develop an atmosphere. Look at how we describe nature:

— an *angry* storm
— a *raging* river
— a *quiet* forest
— *forbidding* mountains
— *gentle* rain

Nature—or its elements—no longer seems remote, untouchable, once we personify and turn it into a character. Think how much easier it is to speak of an "ugly" snowstorm rather than describe a "twenty-two-inch snowfall with the winds blowing heavily and the temperatures hovering around zero. . ." We call it "ugly" or we describe one of its characteristics such as "the swirling, blowing maelstrom" and we give it life.

How would we apply this to our beach scene at dusk? In the first example we see a number of details grouped together, all of them usual on a beach at dusk. In the second paragraph there are elements which one might not find on most beaches, and there has also been no attempt to overload the passage with details. In short, the second example tries to establish the mood by utilizing one or two key details, leaving the reader free to develop an image that seems most comfortable. In the first example, we paint in all the details, and we don't make it especially interesting because there's nothing unusual, or dramatic, in what we've portrayed.

We'll lose readers quickly if we do this again and again.

It needn't happen, though, if we think in terms of drama, instead of fact-reporting. Anton Chekov, perhaps the most accomplished short-story writer of all, provided a simple formula for using nature with any descriptive passage. "It should be brief and have a character of relevance," he wrote, "one ought to seize upon the little particulars, grouping them in such a way that, in reading, when you shut your eyes, you get a picture. . . Nature becomes animated if you are not squeamish about employing comparisons of her phenomena with ordinary human activities. . ."

How about our little boy on the beach? The phenomenon of nature is in the changing colors of the setting sun as reflected by the bottle. . . and the ordinary human activity would be the boy stopping and examining the phenomenon because little boys are curious. Doesn't this create a mood and isn't this more dramatic than leaving nothing to the reader's imagination?

Once we decide how much nature we intend to use in a particular descriptive passage, we have to think about the mood and atmosphere we want to convey. Will it be gloom or joy or peacefulness or agitation or something else? Do we want to use nature to help set this up? For example, do we want nature to act in harmony with the mood of the scene, or do we want it to act in contrast? In short, how can we use nature to make the most dramatic impact on the reader?

If we use it in harmony with the way the characters are feeling, it has the advantage of emphasizing that mood or atmosphere, of making it more impressive. In some instances this would be important indeed.

Take Ed McBain, the prolific mystery and suspense writer. In his novel, *Rumpelstiltskin,* a woman whom his lawyer-hero had been dating was killed. The lawyer prepares to go to her funeral, and McBain describes the weather and its impact:

Wednesday morning dawned cold and gray and bleak. The temperature on the thermometer outside my kitchen window hovered at the thirty-one degree mark, which meant it was one degree below freezing —point five below zero on the Celsius scale. The cable-television forcast from the National Weather Service in Ruskin, Florida, reported winds from the southeast at twenty-seven knots, seas to twelve feet, and a zero possibility of precipitation. Temperatures in the Tricity Area (which included Tampa, Sarasota and Colusa) were expected to rise no higher than the mid- to upper forties. It was altogether a rotten day for a funeral. . .

The mood in this passage is certainly not happy or joyful. The cold, gray day, the winds, the seas all indicate gloom and bleakness. Temperatures at or below the freezing mark mean discomfort, especially in a sunbelt locale such as Florida, and the prospect for improvement during the day isn't reassuring.

It was altogether a rotten day for a funeral. The author characterizes the mood of the day—a rotten day—and weaves it around the major event, a funeral. A harmony of circumstances, really. the weather and the event. The funeral will be sad and gloomy, and weather accentuates that.

Doesn't that make the funeral even sadder? It's a bleak event made bleaker by the weather. And it has the effect of underscoring the event for the reader.

Something the reader will not forget.

Make the weather-atmosphere harmonize with the event-mood, and the event takes on added importance.

It really does.

But there are times we *don't* want harmony; there are times when we want nature to be in contrast to the event-mood.

Why? Because it adds drama and allows characters and events to be more sharply defined.

Take Herman Melville's *Moby Dick,* for example. We know the story—the search for the white whale, obsession and madness and killing and survival. It is a story of the cruel sea and cruel fate, of nature seeking vengeance, and of men finally overwhelmed. The ship is lost, almost all the men are lost, and the whale triumphs. Nature is not kind to the men of the *Pequod*, but in the beginning of the book that is not the way Melville portrays it:

It was a clear steel blue day. The firmaments of air and sea were hardly separable in that all-pervading azure; only, the pensive air was transparently pure and soft, with a woman's look, and the robust and man-like sea heaved with long, strong, lingering swells, as Samson's chest in his sleep.

Hither and thither, on high, glided snow-white wings of small, unspeckled birds; these were the gentle thoughts of the feminine air; but to and fro in the deeps, far down in the' bottomless blue, rushed mighty leviathans, sword-fish and sharks; and these were the strong, troubled, murderous thinkings of the masculine sea. . .

Melville has personified nature—the feminine air and the masculine sea—and this provides a character for the story. Nature becomes all powerful and ultimately destroys men and ship, providing a sharp contrast in mood to the gentler attitude the author takes in the beginning of the story. At first, the sky and the air and the sea are painted in kind tones (the only untoward note is when Melville refers to the sea as having "troubled, murderous thinkings"), and we get the feeling that nature will accentuate and sustain the search for the white whale.

But no. The gentle sea, the kind air, the azure sky become roaring areas of conflict where the mood of the whaling ship —and its sailors—shows suspicion, fury, greed, cruelty, madness. The serenity of nature that Melville depicts in the beginning of the book is in sharp contrast to the atmosphere surrounding the whaling expedition, once things get underway.

Does it help to do it this way? The gentle sea and the urge to kill whales. . . the balmy air and the cruel obsession for the white whale. . . the calm sky and the prayers for a successful whale hunt. . . These contrasts with nature and the mood of the event give the entire story a starker reality than if nature were the personification of evil, because nature becomes a silent, almost disapproving witness to what is happening.

These events are occuring on *my* gentle sea? They are tearing through *my* balmy air, *my* serene sky?

How awful!

How dramatic, we writers would say!

Nature is more than sea and air and sky, of course. It is mountains and rivers and rocks and anything that might be growing in, under or on top of the earth. Nature provides us with a setting that can create a mood or atmosphere that will certainly influence the storyline.

For example, we come upon a natural cave, we enter it and suddenly we're in a huge underground amphitheatre; the air is clammy, strange shadows dart across the cave walls, there are unexplained clicking noises from somewhere. Large crystals hang from the ceiling, and a tiny rivulet of water meanders across the powdery floor. . .

Nature (the cave) has set up a mood or atmosphere (most likely suspenseful), and the story will proceed from here. But note it is *nature* which has created the setting. From that the mood or atmosphere develops.

All of us can think of nature in many forms, but see the choices Leonard Lutwack offers in his book *The Role of Place in Literature:*

Vegetation has a most important influence on the quality of places. Vegetation is life, and its degree of density indicates the amount of life a place harbors. Places devoid of plant life are associated with deprivation and death, places of abundant vegetation are pleasant and erotic. Deserts and mountain tops present the terrifying aspects of lifeless matter whereas the forest is life in an active, wild state. . .

What he means, of course, is that the lusher the setting, the livelier the storyline and the livelier the mood and atmosphere. As we saw in Chapter Nine, there are times when we wish to contrast one with the other, but generally he is correct. It is a common technique for the lushness of the setting to influence, if not control, the drama that will take place.

See the following passage from Knut Hamsun's *Growth of the Soil* (which many feel won him the Nobel Prize), the story of Isak who plods the valleys and mountain tops of Norway seeking a place to settle. Isak is alone and one night he settles on a high slope overlooking a valley and goes to sleep.

The morning shows him a range of pasture and woodland. He moves down, and there is a green hillside; far below, a glimpse of the stream, and a hare bounding across. The man nods his head, as it were, approvingly—the stream is not so broad but that a hare may cross it at a bound. A white grouse sitting close upon its nest starts up at his feet with an

angry hiss and he nods again; feathered game and fur
—a good spot this. Heather, bilberry and cloudberry
cover the ground; there are tiny ferns, and the seven-
pointed star flowers of the wintergreen. Here and
there he stops to dig with an iron tool, and finds good
mould, or peaty soil, manured with the rotted wood
and fallen leaves of a thousand years. He nods, to say
he has found himself a place to stay and live. . .

And live he does. He develops a homestead, finds a wife,
has children and spends the next fifty years farming his land.
The theme of the book is. . . life out of the living earth. . .
and the mood and atmosphere are of a farm family struggling
and surviving and building a life.

But note Hamsun's depiction of the land that Isak has
found. It is lush and promising and vital—all the things he
would need to make his farming and his life a success. The
rich land, then, provides a lively background for Isak to build
a family and for his family to grow and prosper. . .

In short, the lush surroundings make it possible for Hamsun to develop Isak and the storyline so that the mood and atmosphere of the book are of life and liveliness, of deep
pleasure and strong emotion.

Nature lives!

And so will the story.

21

The Music of Words

From time to time we've mentioned the way words sound, that they tickle the ear as well as the mind, that this is something every writer has to make allowance for. We deal in images, of course, but the words we produce must appeal to a reader's senses, and those senses are what form the images.

We "hear" the words of D.H. Lawrence portray the heavy movements of a team of draught horses in his story, *The Horse Dealer's Daughter:*

> They were tied head to tail, four of them, and they heaved along to where a lane branched off from the highroad, planting their great hoofs floutingly in the fine black mud, swinging their great rounded haunches sumptuously, and trotting a few sudden steps as they were led into the lane, round the corner. . .

Read this aloud. . . emphasize the image-making words: *heaved. . .planting. . .floutingly. . .swinging. . .sumptuously. . .trotting.* . . Don't we "hear" the crinkle of the leather harnesses, the snorts of the horses, the clop-clop of their hoofs, even the sharp commands of those leading them?

We "hear" the words. Our senses are affected. An atmosphere is created.

And if we take it a step further, we could probably "smell" the musky horse odor and be warmed by the majesty of the horse team as it passed.

But it is the sounds of the words that are key, and we must understand that these word-sounds produce images in our reader's mind. We should strive to establish that these are the images we *want* the reader to acquire.

These word-sounds are what we call the "music" of words because they do what a violin solo or piano riff or clarinet pizzicato does. . . they create a sensory reaction whether it's euphoria or gloom or tension. They make us "feel" the sounds, and this provides true involvement in mood and atmosphere.

To some extent we must think as the poet does, using poetic devices such as simile, metaphor, assonance and alliteration. Image-making is what we're after, and these do help:

— ". . . the simple succor of serenity surprised him. ."
— ". . . he survived as the turtle survives, retreating to an inner fortress and waiting it out. . .
— ". . . she sailed the sea of hope. . ."

Never forget that what we try to do is establish a mood or atmosphere through the word-sounds we develop. There must be a connection between them. . . Suppose we wanted

190

to create a scene of euphoria. We certainly wouldn't use words or phrases portraying gloom or sadness:

— . . . the gray-like walls pulsated with the uneven
   sounds of happiness. . .

Doesn't work, does it?

And we wouldn't want harsh word-sounds in an atmosphere of softness and gentleness:

— . . . she cooed at the baby, clucking her tongue
   and sucking her teeth. . .

This doesn't work either.

Now see something that does work. Here's a passage from Doris Lessing's story *A Sunrise on the Veld*. A young fifteen-year-old African boy is getting up to go hunting by himself, and we see how the words fit so nicely in the pre-dawn atmosphere:

The boy stretched his frame full-length, touching the
wall at his head with his hands, and the bedfoot with
his toes; then he sprang out, like a fish leaping from
water. And it was cold, cold.

He always dressed rapidly, so as to try and conserve
his night-warmth till the sun rose two hours later; but
by the time he had on his clothes his hands were
numbed and he could scarcely hold his shoes. These
he did not put on for fear of waking his parents, who
never came to know how easily he rose.

As soon as he stepped over the lintel, the flesh of
his soles contracted on the chilled earth, and his legs
began to ache with cold. . .

Think of the hours before dawn. What comes to mind? Darkness, ominous stillness, chill and cold. . . a variety of unsettling circumstances. Generally, this is a time of watchfulness, of waiting, and if we are going to portray these feelings in a few well-spotted words or phrases, how would it be done?

— . . . And it was cold, cold

— . . . his hands were numbed. . .

— . . . he could scarcely hold his shoes. . .

— . . . the flesh of his soles contracted

— . . . his legs began to ache with cold. . .

Don't we get the sense of his physical discomfort while we also grasp the broader sweep of an unsettled atmosphere? He's cold and uncomfortable, but out there, in the night, the ominous day awaits. Is he prepared for it?

Cold, numbed, chilled. . . these are words that produce sounds. Try them aloud. . . they resonate with discomfort even as they describe the boy's physical condition and provide a clue to the story atmosphere.

Note, too, the poetic simile: ". . . he sprang out, like a fish leaping from water. . ."

The music of words. Poetic, sensory, atmospheric.

Sometimes an entire passage can ring with poetic touches, and the words can sweep before us with the broadest musicality. One of these is from a story by Conrad Aiken, *Silent Snow, Secret Snow,* where the protaganist lies in bed waiting for the postman.

He wanted to hear him come round the corner. And that was precisely the joke—he never did. He never came. He never had come—*round the corner*—again. For when at last the steps *were* heard, they had already, he was quite sure, come a little down the hill, to the first house; and even so, the steps were curiously different—they were softer, they had a new secrecy about them, they were muffled and indistinct; and while the rhythm of them was the same, it now said a new thing—it said peace, it said remoteness, it said cold, it said sleep...

Notice the rhythm here, the cadence repeated over and over, the same word, the same verb form. All of this phrasing describes the *sound* of the postman's step so that the reader can form an image which will then establish a mood and atmosphere. See how many ways the sounds come:

— they were softer
— they had a new secrecy about them
— they were muffled and indistinct
— the rhythm of them said peace
— the rhythm of them said remoteness
— the rhythm of them said cold
— the rhythm of them said sleep

What do the sounds mean?

That it snowed during the night. Instead of describing the snow, Aiken has us see it as it affects the steps of the postman. In doing this he creates a much more intense image in our minds because we can visualize the sounds, and from them we can imagine the scene.

The sounds of the postman. . . are music, really.

The important thing is that the sounds convey an image or put us into a mood or establish an atmosphere. We think of music as a pleasing experience, by and large, because it is supposed to appeal to our senses. But, of course, music doesn't always have to be lyrical or melodic or even uplifting so long as it moves us in some direction.

The same is true with words. The sounds they convey don't have to establish a pleasurable image or even a respectable one, so long as they establish *something*! Just as with music, word-sounds have to move us in a direction that will create an image which will, in turn, set a mood.

For example, we can use unhappy-sounding words: *gross. . . sweat-filled. . . whining. . . oozed. . . soured. . . smog. . .* and we set up a distasteful image which will then establish an unpleasant mood or atmosphere. *Yet this may be exactly what we intend to do* because our story demands it. Don't, therefore, think only in terms of happy sounds or beautiful word-music. Use the sounds to establish a mood or an atmosphere consistent with the story.

Just as Tom Wolfe does in his novel *The Bonfire of the Vanities.* The setting is a chi-chi dinner party in midtown Manhattan, and the host is giving a little talk to the dinner guests about his pleasure in their company. He mentions one of the guests, Bobby Shaflett, known as the "Golden Hillbilly," an opera star of some renown. The host continues:

"I mean, sometimes we ask Bobby to come over just so we can listen to his *laugh.* Bobby's laugh is music, far as I'm concerned—besides, we never get him to sing for us, even when Inez plays the piano!"

Hack hack hack hack hack hack hack hack went Inez Bavardage. *Haw haw haw haw haw haw haw haw,* the Golden Hillbilly drowned her out with a laugh of his own. It was an amazing laugh, this one. *Haw haw haww hawww hawwww hawwwww hawwwwww,* it rose and rose and rose, and then it broke into a sob. The room froze—dead silence—for that instant it took the diners, or most of them, to realize they had just heard the famous laughing sob of "Vesti la giubba" aria from *Pagliacci. . .*

These word-sounds aren't particularly pretty—at least until we get to the aria—but they do ring through our ears, don't they? Wolfe is describing a laugh, not with adjectives (such as "loud" or "harsh" or "squeaky") but by the way it hits our ears. "Haw haw" brings it to us in its most natural, direct manner, it is not the characterization of the sound but the sound itself. "Haw haw haw. . ." may not be musical in the conventional sense but it produces the word-wound that will establish the mood and the atmosphere for the story.

Read this passage aloud. Go ahead. . . Don't the sounds give a clear image of the person—whether Inez or the Golden Hillbilly? Inez doesn't sound attractive does she? Is this the image Wolfe wants to produce? If it isn't why, then, let us "hear" her laugh?

The mood and the atmosphere of the dinner party, of course, are what Wolfe is trying to portray, and by appealing to our sense of hearing, he shows us that some dinner parties are sillier than others, that some people for all their wordly goods and veneer of sophistication remain unattractive, even ridiculous. He uses the actual sounds of words to make us see things that other writers attempt to portray with adjectives and adverbs.

It is the music of the solo instrument rather than the symphony of an orchestra.

Does it work?

Mmmmmmmmmmmmmmmm. . .

Sure does.

Bibliography

Books

Bement, Douglas. *Weaving the Short Story*. New York: Farrar and Rinehart Inc., 1931.

Bowen, Elizabeth. *Collected Impressions*. New York: Alfred A. Knopf, 1950.

Bruccoli, Mathew J., editorial director. *Conversations with Writers I*. Detroit: Gale Research Co., 1977.

Burroway, Janet. *Writing Fiction*. Boston: Little Brown and Co, 1982.

Clark, Glenn. *A Manual of the Short Story Art*. New York: The MacMillan Co., 1923.

Curry, Peggy Simson. *Creating Fiction From Experience*. Boston: The Writer Inc., 1964.

Eastman, Richard M. *A Guide to the Novel*. Scranton: Chandler Publishing, 1965,.

Fensch, Thomas. *The Hardest Parts*. Austin: Lander Moore Books, 1984.

Frederick, John T. *A Handbook of Short Story Writing*. New York: Alfred A. Knopf, 1924.

Gardner, John. *The Art of Fiction*. New York: Alfred A. Knopf, 1984.

Gordon, Caroline. *How to Read a Novel*. New York: Viking, 1953.

Hamilton, Clayton. *Manual of the Art of Fiction*. Garden City; Doubleday, Page and Co., 1918.

Lutwack, Leonard. *The Role of Place in Literature*. Syracuse: Syracuse University Press, 1984.

Macauley, Robie and Lanning, George. *Technique In Fiction*. New York: Harper and Row, 1964.

Madden, David. *A Primer of the Novel For Readers and Writers*. Metuchen: Scarecrow Press Inc., 1980.

Noble, June and William. *Steal This Plot*. Middlebury: Paul S. Eriksson, 1985.

Noble, William. *"Shut Up!" He Explained*. Middlebury: Paul S. Eriksson, 1987.

Sloane, William. *The Craft of Writing*. New York: W. W. Norton and Co., 1979.

Uzzell, Thomas. *Narrative Technique*. New York: Harcourt Brace and Co., 1923.

Vivante, Arturo. *Writing Fiction*. Boston: The Writer Inc., 1980.

Zinsser, William. *On Writing Well*. New York: Harper & Row Inc., 1976.

Articles

Aldrich, R.S. "Writing Action Scenes." *The Writer*. February, 1981.

Block, Lawrence. "Details, Details." *Writer's Digest*, December, 1984.

Block, Lawrence. "View Finder." *Writer's Digest*, November, 1982.

Chamberlain, A. "When Scenery Becomes Character." *The Writer*, August, 1981.

Elliott, Sumner Locke. "Against Nostalgia." *The Writer*, February, 1988.

Elmblad, Mary. "A Sense of Place." *The Writer*, October, 1987.

Erdrich, Louise. "Where I Ought to Be: a writer's sense of place." *New York Times Book Review*, July 28, 1985.

Franco, M. "Making a Scene." *The Writer*, June, 1982.

Freer, Marjorie Mueller. "Developing the Eye of the Writer." *Writer's Digest*, July, 1987.

Haukeness, Helen. "Setting Your Novel Straight." *Writer's Digest*, December, 1984.

Markus, J. "On Location." *The Writer*, June, 1987.

Masterton, G. "Being There." *The Writer*, August, 1985.

Naylor, P.R. "Mood Plot and Theme." *The Writer,* March, 1986.

Provost, Gary. "The Hidden Work of Words." *Writer's Digest,* July, 1981.

Reece, Coleen L. "Ankle Deep in Warm Tears: How to Make Nostalgia Pay." *Writer's Digest,* October, 1980.

Rockwell, F.A. "Making the Scene." *Handbook of Short Story Writing.* Ed. Frank A. Dickson and Sandra Smythe. *Writer's Digest,* Cincinnati, Ohio, 1970.

Sorrels, Roy and Daniel, Megan, "Decoding the Secrets of Selling Popular Fiction." *Writer's Digest,* April, 1981.

Sorrels, Roy ("R"). "The Sensuous Writer." *Writer's Digest,* March, 1986.

Stewart, Mary. "Setting and Background in the Novel." *Writing Mystery and Crime Fiction.* Ed. Sylvia K. Burack. The Writer Inc., Boston, 1985.

Stillman, Peter R. "A Writer's Potpourri." *1986 Fiction Writer's Market.* ed. Jean M. Fredette. Writer's Digest Books, Cincinnati, Ohio, 1986.

Williamson, J.N. "Scare Tactics—the Guts and Bolts of Horror Writing." *1986 Fiction Writer's Market.* Ed. Jean M. Fredette. Writer's Digest Books, Cincinnati, Ohio, 1986.

Index